A missionary preaching to sailors on board the Oiseau

THE CHEVALIER DE CHAUMONT
AND
THE ABBÉ DE CHOISY

ASPECTS OF THE EMBASSY TO SIAM 1685

THE CHEVALIER DE CHAUMONT

AND

THE ABBÉ DE CHOISY

ASPECTS OF THE EMBASSY TO SIAM 1685

being

Alexandre de Chaumont
Relation of the Embassy to Siam 1685

and

François-Timoléon de Choisy
Memoranda on religion and commerce in Siam
and
Reflections on the Embassy to Siam

Edited
and in part translated by

MICHAEL SMITHIES

SILKWORM BOOKS
Chiang Mai

Some other books by Michael Smithies

The Siamese Memoirs of Count Claude de Forbin 1685-1688
Alexander Hamilton: A Scottish Sea Captain in Southeast Asia 1689-1723
Abbé de Choisy: Journal of a Voyage to Siam, 1685–1686
A Thai Boyhood
Bight of Bangkok
Descriptions of Old Siam
Discovering Thailand (with Achille Clarac)
Old Bangkok
The Cultural Sites of Burma, Thailand, and Cambodia (with Jacques Dumarçay)
The Discourses at Versailles of the First Siamese Ambassadors to France
The Siamese Embassy to the Sun King: The Personal Memoirs of Kosa Pan
Yogyakarta, Cultural Heart of Indonesia
A Javanese Boyhood
A Singapore Boyhood
A Busy Week: Tales of Today's Thailand
***

First published in 1997 by
Silkworm Books
54/1 Sridonchai Road, Chiang Mai 50100, Thailand.
E-mail: silkworm@pobox.com

Silkworm Books is a registered trade mark of
Trasvin Publications Limited Partnership.

Cover design by T. Jittidejarak
Set in 11 pt. Palatino
Endpapers: After Tachard, Guy, A barge with 120 rowers,
Voyage au Siam des Pères Jésuites envoyés par le Roi aux Indes et à la Chine

Printed by O.S. Printing House, Bangkok.

CONTENTS

ABBÉ DE CHOISY:
Three texts relating to the embassy to Siam 1685

ILLUSTRATIONS

Line drawings by Jacques Dumarçay, consultant architect of the Ecole Française d'Extrême Orient

PREFACE AND ACKNOWLEDGEMENTS

The Chevalier de Chaumont's account of his embassy to Siam has been unobtainable in English for more than three hundred years, and, while the Abbé de Choisy's journal of his voyage to Siam in 1685-6 first appeared in English in 1993, his recollections of the embassy written later in life, which appeared in two different books, one published just before his death in 1724, and one shortly after, have never to our knowledge appeared in English. Choisy's two confidential memoranda, written on his return journey from Siam and dealing with religion in Siam and commerce in the region, only appeared in complete form for the first time in French in 1995, and consequently also appear here for the first time in English.

These two very different characters were complimentary, and so are their texts, and their publication here is intended to assist those interested in learning more about the extraordinary French adventure in Siam in the seventeenth century and who do not have a sufficient command of French to master the texts in the original.

As ever, my thanks must go to Professor Dirk Van der Cruysse, who first brought to my attention the text in Choisy's *Histoire de l'Eglise Vol. XI* dealing with Siam, and who first published Choisy's memoranda on commerce, and on religion in complete form. He has also helped with an interpretation of a phrase of Choisy, and Jacques Roman has similarly helped with an ambiguous passage in Chaumont. Jacques Dumarçay very kindly provided the original drawings to illustrate this text. Michel Jacq-Hergoualc'h has, as usual, been kindness itself in checking on early editions in Paris of Chaumont, and, while others have helped in different ways, only I (or gremlins in the printery) am responsible for any errors which might appear here.

I first became interested in the texts concerning the 1685 French embassy to Siam when teaching in the University of Hong Kong twenty-five years ago, and started collecting different versions of them with a view to publishing them eventually. Only in retirement has this project become a possibility. It has been a long wait, but I hope the reader will find it worthwhile.

Michael Smithies
Bua Yai
December 1995

Loading supplies en route for Siam

INTRODUCTION

The apparently bizarre involvement of France in Siam in the years 1685-1688 needs some explanation today.

French missionaries had first arrived in Ayutthaya in 1662 and were much impressed with the religious tolerance in the country; they were free to preach and convert at will, as was anyone else. The fact that they made few conversions was, in their eyes, neither here nor there; Rome was not propagated in a day. Louis XIV, 'His Most Christian Majesty', was a strong supporter of missionary efforts, still more so after 1683, under the influence of his devout and secret wife Madame de Maintenon and his Jesuit confessor, Father de La Chaize. Already in 1659 he had assisted in the foundation of the Société des Missions Etrangères (in this text their members are capitalized as Missionaries). Pope Alexander VII was persuaded to nominate French bishops to defunct sees, and gave them the title of apostolic vicars, a move hopefully calculated to avert the wrath of the Portuguese who had been given the job (which by the late seventeenth century they were clearly incapable of performing) of Christianizing the Indies under the Padroado, the division of the new world between Spain and Portugal in the Treaty of Tordesillas of 1494. The first such bishop, Lambert de La Motte, came to Siam in 1662, and died in Ayutthaya in 1679. Louis Laneau, Bishop of Metellopolis, was given his episcopal title and created apostolic vicar of Siam in 1673; a saintly man by all accounts, he had to suffer the indignities of imprisonment and the dispersal of his tiny flock when the French were forced to withdraw from Siam in 1688.

But it was not the apparently rich pickings in missionary endeavour alone that attracted the French to Siam in the second half of the seventeenth century. France was a very late, and not noticeably successful aspirant for the richer material pickings obtained from trade with the Indies. The English East India Company was incorporated in London in 1600, and two years later its Dutch counterpart, the VOC, was set up. These were fierce rivals and it was not until the following century that their different spheres of influence were largely established, though by no means agreed. The French started an East India Company in 1604, but it lapsed, and was revived by Richelieu in 1642. This also collapsed, and in 1664 Colbert established the Compagnie des Indes Orientales with a monopoly over Eastern trade for fifty years.

But while the Dutch and the English were trading with Siam from the beginning of the century, the French did not appear on the scene until 1680. Commercial relations were established then by the representative of the French Indies Company, André Deslandes-Boureau, who came trading in the *Vautour*, which was in Siamese waters from 3 September to 24 December, giving time enough to present gifts to the *Phra Klang* from the Company and draw up a general trading treaty.

King Narai, on the Siamese throne since 1656, was anxious to have a possible ally against the predatory and powerfully entrenched Dutch traders, mindful of the blockade the Dutch had effected at the mouth of Chao Phya in 1663. The Dutch had an important trading house or "factory" in Ayutthaya, another called Amsterdam near the mouth of the river, and yet another for the export of tin at Ligor (Nakhon Si Thammarat). They were solidly established in Batavia since 1619, had taken Malacca from the Portuguese in 1641, and were poised to take over the one remaining independent regional trading centre of importance at Bantam in 1682. The only other Western traders of consequence in the region, the English, had opened and closed their trading house in Ayutthaya too often to be serious contenders for royal favour.

Doubtless with the encouragement of the Bishop of Metellopolis, and responding to the good relations Deslandes-Boureau managed to establish, King Narai decided to send an embassy to France. This, led by Phya Pipat Kosa, and seconded by Luang Sri Wisan and Khun Nakhon Vichai, taking fifty bales of presents, left on the *Vautour* at the end of 1680 and transshipped, after a long stay, at Bantam onto the *Soleil d'Orient* which called at Mauritius in November 1681 and was never heard of again. It was presumed sunk in a storm off Madagascar at the end of the year. In 1683 Mgr Laneau informed King Narai of the presumed shipwreck, and the king decided to send two envoys (they were not formally credited with the title of ambassadors) to France to enquire about the fate of his embassy. With them went Father Bénigne Vachet, one of the French Missionaries working under Mgr Laneau, as interpreter.

They arrived in France via England at the beginning of October 1684. It cannot be said that they were successful envoys; they were uncouth and refused to socialize, much to the chagrin of Vachet. He had few connections with the great and powerful, but a person then staying in the Missions Etrangères, recovering from an illness, was Abbé François-Timoléon de Choisy (1644-1724), who knew everyone at court; his intriguing mother was even rumoured to

3

have given her favours to the king when young, and her son had been a youthful playmate of Monsieur, Louis XIV's younger brother, Philippe d'Orléans. Choisy arranged for the envoys to be presented 'informally' at Versailles (they much irritated the king because they refused to rise from the floor in his presence) and for Vachet to meet the king's confessor, Father de La Chaize. Vachet took the opportunity to imply that King Narai was interested in other religions, which was true, for he was intellectually curious, and might be persuaded, if a sufficiently important embassy were sent to him, to convert to Christianity, which was not true at all. The idea of converting an Eastern potentate to Catholicism clearly flattered Louis XIV, who agreed to send such an embassy to Siam.

Choisy, who was well known at court for his wit, his gambling debts and his transvestite exploits, had high hopes, when he heard that an embassy was being considered for Siam, of being made ambassador. He was pipped at the post; the Marquis de Seignelay, Secretary of State for the Navy, informed him the king had already approved the appointment of Chaumont.

The Chevalier Alexandre de Chaumont (?1640-1710) came from one of the oldest French families. He counted among his ancestors knights who had taken part in the Crusades to defend the kingdom of Jerusalem, and a chamberlain who took part in the siege of Orléans and the consecration of Charles VII at Reims. His brother Hugues was a marshal of the king's armies, his uncle Jean was librarian and keeper of Henri IV's medals, and a cousin, Abbé Paul Philippe de Chaumont, was a member of the Académie Française from 1654. His family had embraced the reform and become Protestant, but he and his brothers converted over time to Catholicism.

Father Guy Tachard, who accompanied Chaumont to Siam in 1685, has this to say of him:

This gentleman is known throughout the kingdom for his particular merit and the nobility of his most ancient and illustrious family. From birth and during his early years he was committed to the Calvinist heresy, but God gave him the grace to abandon it, together with his brothers, who converted one after the other at different times. The youngest of all, after having served for a long time in the army and gaining the reputation of a brave gentleman and good officer, weary of the world, and touched by the desire to work for his salvation, entered our Company [of Jesus] where he lived and died a saintly life, having edified all those who knew him by rare examples of all kinds of virtues, and particularly by heroic patience when faced with the great discomfort which his wounds, received during war service, caused.

The Chevalier de Chaumont, of whom we are now speaking, was his eldest brother, and began his service on land where his marked merit signalled him for the particular esteem of the still young king [Louis XIV]. He was then sent to Toulon to command the Marines, and to train them in all the necessary exercises for gentlemen who were destined to command His Majesty's vessels. He was subsequently made a ship's captain, and major-general of the king's naval armies in the Levant. His zeal for the service of his king in no way diminished the continual application he gave to the service of God, and everyone rightly considered him as a man of singular wisdom and piety. It is for this that His Majesty, who was chiefly concerned for the well-being of religion, and the conversion of the King of Siam, in the embassy he was proposing to send, chose the Chevalier de Chaumont for such a glorious task, persuaded by the good example he would offer to that country, giving so many proofs of the holiness of Christianity, that they would succeed in convincing the king of the truth of our religion. (Guy Tachard, *Voyage au Siam des Pères Jésuites...*, 1686: 9-10)

While Chaumont might have the appropriate religious background, his military career did not obviously make him a good ambassador for such a delicate mission as converting the King of Siam; as Gatty (1963:xiv) points out, "he was more used to giving orders and being obeyed than discussing clauses and treaties". He was pious to a degree, unbending, excessively imbued with his importance as ambassador of Louis XIV, and forever standing on his dignity.

When Choisy heard that Chaumont had been appointed ambassador, he changed tack, pointing out the length of the journey and the unknown dangers of the embassy, how it would be better to have a second in command should the ambassador fall sick or die, and how it might be necessary to stay on in Siam to instruct the king in the mysteries of the Christian faith in order to achieve his conversion. Louis XIV somewhat grudgingly approved Choisy's appointment as coadjutant ambassador, saying at the same time that he had never heard of the post before. Choisy's enthusiasm for Siam should be seen partly as result of a decision to reform, subsequent to his serious illness (he took orders when in Siam), and partly to escape the confines of Paris and his creditors.

The two ships, the *Oiseau* and the *Maligne,* carrying the embassy and the royal presents left Brest in March 1685, with the returning Siamese envoys, Vachet and two fellow Missionaries, Basset and Manuel, and a host of other clerics on board. Tachard, already mentioned, was one of six Jesuits going to China, there was an independent traveller, the Abbé de Chayla, Chaumont took his personal almoner the Abbé Jully and a ship's almoner. He also took as secretary the Sieur de La Brosse-Bonneau (a brother of André Deslandes-Boureau), and the Sieur de Billy as his maître d'hôtel (who was later promoted to be governor of Junk Ceylon, that is Phuket, and imprisoned by the Siamese after the French surrender and departure in 1688). The embassy arrived in Siam on 23 September, and departed on 22 December, returning to France on 18 June 1686, with a full-blown Siamese embassy headed by Kosa Pan, with a deputy and assistant ambassador, a number of secretaries, and 300 bales of presents for the court, for the most part selected by Choisy.

Between the departure of the first Siamese embassy to France in 1680 and the mission which left Siam in January 1684 to establish what had become of this, a new factor had emerged in the political and trading scene in Ayutthaya, in the form of the person called by the French 'Monsieur Constance', that is the Levantine adventurer from Cephalonia, Konstantin Gherakis, which family name he transformed into the westernized form of Phaulkon. This is not the place to go into details concerning his early life, much of which is obscure and sometimes contradictory. Suffice it to say that from being in a lowly position on the East India Company's boats, he came to Siam working for some of the Company's officials, entered the service of the *Phra Klang* Kosathibodi, and probably in 1683, the same year as his patron's disgrace (the two events appear to be connected), into that of King Narai. Thereafter his power appears almost untrammelled; though he accepted no formal high office from the king, he was effectively in charge of the government of the country's external relations and trade. Well aware of the envy his position as chief confident and minister of the king caused, he was keen to bolster his position, which was entirely dependent on the whim and good health of King Narai. Phaulkon appears to have conceived of a plan to bring immigrants to Siam, who would be Catholics like himself (he converted in 1682 under Jesuit influence), and would allow him to continue to wield power by proxy should the king die. His enemies—and he had many—said that he planned to become king himself, but, while Phaulkon was often drunk with power, he was not blind to realities, and the idea of a foreigner becoming King of Siam was an inherently untenable proposition.

If the chief reason, in Louis XIV's eyes, for sending his embassy in 1685 to Siam was to convert King Narai, then Chaumont failed dismally. He was certainly sent on no further diplomatic missions after his return from Siam; he received a pension of 1,200 *livres* and died in 1710. The only testimony to his journey was his *Relation de l'Ambassade de Mr le Chevalier de Chaumont à la Cour du Roy de Siam* published by Seneuze and Horthemels in Paris in 1686. This quickly went through two more editions in Paris, one in the same year and one in 1687, and a pirated Amsterdam edition with Mortier was also published in 1686. A German edition appeared in Frankfurt in 1687, a Dutch edition the same year in Amsterdam; an Italian edition also appeared in that year, as did an English edition in London. There appear to have been no further editions in any language, apart from the photocopied version of the French text produced by Chalermnit in Bangkok in 1985 (unfortunately this does not indicate which edition was used; it seems to have been the third Paris edition of 1687, but only reproduces nineteen of the twenty-nine pages listing the presents brought back from Siam, and omits the ten pages of directions taken and distances covered on the return journey).

The reasons for the lack of further interest in Chaumont's text are not hard to find. It was a very succinct account, not always accurate in its observations, and said almost nothing about the discussions concerning his mission while in Siam. In spite of the enormous interest in all things Siamese from the time of the arrival in France in 1686 of the Siamese embassy, Chaumont's text was overtaken by more detailed works about the country, like those of Tachard, cited above, of 1686, complete with 30 plates, Gervaise *(Histoire naturelle et politique du Royaume de Siam*, 1688), Choisy *(Journal du voyage de Siam*, 1687), and above all La Loubère *(Du Royaume de Siam*, 1691), as well as the numerous texts relating to the so-called revolution in Siam (which might perhaps be better called the Lopburi coup) of 1688.

Chaumont so eschews detailed information and personal insights that his brevity is more appropriate to a ship's log, and his text indeed becomes a log towards the end, with pages giving the directions and distances covered of the return journey from Siam to Brest (as they are of no interest today, they have been omitted in this edition). The lists of presents brought back from Siam also puff out the final pages of the text; the anonymous English translator had the honesty to admit he was 'weary of relating' them and gave up half-way. But these lists are of specialist interest, for they show the kind of objects arriving at or occasionally being made in Siam, and which were thought worthy of presenting to members of the royal family and ministers at Versailles; that they were barely appreciated is another matter (see Smithies, 1986).

For all that, Chaumont was the head of the embassy, and so his account had the imprint of authority. He occasionally has details which the other accounts of the embassy lack, notably the presence in Ayutthaya of a small Armenian colony of Christian families, mostly serving in King Narai's horseguard, the people left behind in Siam on the departure of his embassy, and above all the very precise recording of the goods imported to Siam from the different countries in the region and the exports from Siam in return to these territories. Yet Chaumont was not the best informed of envoys; his listing of the provinces of Siam seems to have come directly from a text of Jacques de Bourges published in 1666 and itself wrong. He was clearly fascinated, like most Westerners, by the 'Princess Queen' of Siam, whom neither he nor any Western man saw; the whiff of possible incest as well as mystery surrounding the unnamed Krom Luang Yothathep obviously caught even Chaumont's somewhat limited imagination.

In today's parlance, Chaumont was so buttoned up that even five months after the outward journey he had never discussed his mission with his coadjutant ambassador, the effusive and amusing Abbé de Choisy, who, in his posthumous *Mémoires pour servir à l'Histoire de Louis XIV*, wrote:

> *This began to tire me. I foresaw that if this continued, I would count for nothing in Siam, when, through the partition which separated my cabin from his, I heard him pondering over his discourse [for the day of audience]. I said to him a week later (for he continued with the same song) that I had heard the most splendid things in the world. Upon that he took me into his cabin and repeated it to me: I found it faultless. From that day on, he began to speak to me about what had to be done in that country; I gave him my humble opinions. He is a goodly man, and truly a person of means and standing, but he does not know geometry [i.e. he is not well versed]. I did not have much trouble in letting him understand that, as it happened, I could be useful to him in some degree. From that day on he did not even spit without warning me first.* (1983: 146)

Even King Narai's powerful minister, the arriviste

Phaulkon, was intimidated by Chaumont. Choisy recorded on 15 November 1685:

> *A few days ago, the king, when talking to Mr Constance, asked him if he often had discussions with the ambassador [Chaumont]. Mr Constance replied that he did, and still more often with me, because His Excellency had a position to maintain which prevented familiarity.* (1993: 193)

But Chaumont's embassy came to nothing. He returned with a worthless treaty on religion, the terms of which were never even made public in Siam (for the good reason that Phaulkon, who had negotiated for the Siamese, was afraid of the uproar their publication would cause among the profoundly Buddhist populace), and a treaty concerning commerce between France and Siam, which Versailles was to consider less advantageous than that negotiated by Deslandes-Boureau in 1680. It is true neither Chaumont nor Choisy had any trading background, and the French factor at Siam, Véret, was a Parisian jeweller of little consequence or experience. But King Narai, under Phaulkon's influence, had turned trader and established royal monopolies, profitable in the short term, which excluded foreign merchants. The times had changed, and the period of the declining importance of Siam in regional entrepôt trade had begun.

If Chaumont sank into oblivion on his return, apart from the publication of his *Relation*, this was not the case of Choisy. He produced his own eminently readable account in 1687 of the embassy in the form of a daily journal, and in the same year two works on religion. These were sufficient to get him elected to the Académie Française in August 1687; he continued to write prolifically, publishing an eleven volume *Histoire de l'Eglise*, the last volume of which contains a section on his Siamese period, and working intermittently on his *Mémoires pour servir à l'Histoire de Louis XIV*, which also deals with the intrigues of Tachard in the Siamese adventure, and of the arrival of the Siamese ambassadors in France. The work remained unfinished at his death, by when he was dean of the French Academy.

Events subsequent to the embassy are sufficiently well known to warrant no more than the briefest summary here. The Siamese embassy which went with the returning French envoys to France in 1686 was a huge social success, but negotiations took place behind Kosa Pan's back between the Jesuit Tachard, the king's confessor Father de La Chaize, and the Marquis de Seignelay. The result was a further embassy, led by La Loubère, seconded by Céberet, in 1687, with whom the Siamese envoys returned. La Loubère's mission (made more difficult by the unhelpful interventions of Tachard, drunk with self-importance) was closer to a military expedition, and had secret orders to seize the forts at Bangkok and Mergui if they were not handed over voluntarily. The Siamese nobles, led by Petracha, decided to act against the increasing foreign presence in their country, and this led to the coup d'état of 18 May 1688. King Narai, already sick, was kept prisoner in his palace in Lopburi until he died in July, his adopted protégé was beheaded, Phaulkon was tortured and murdered, the king's two half-brothers were killed, and his daughter forced to marry the usurper Petracha, who was crowned king on 1 August. The French troops, led by the buffoon General Desfarges, were besieged in their fort in Bangkok until their ignominious withdrawal was arranged on 13 November; a half-hearted occupation of Phuket took place from 1689-90, after which the French withdrew entirely, Desfarges being recalled, undoubtedly to face a court martial and hanging if he had not had the good fortune to die at sea en route.

So that the entire French adventure came to nothing, and the Missionaries, in whose support intervention started, were imprisoned, their minute flock dispersed, and after the initial Siamese fury had died down, the Mission gradually withered close to extinction in the eighteenth century.

Chaumont's text, therefore, which has not been published in English since 1687 (and has only appeared once in French since then), is not without its value in the documentation of the period. The present editor at first considered publishing the 1687 English translation of Chaumont in its entirety, incorporating deviations from the French original as necessary. But in comparing the two texts it became clear there were more than 450 omissions or mistranslations, and as the result of combining the two texts was not harmonious even if it were scholarly, this approach was abandoned. What is given here, then, is the contemporary English translation where it is reasonably accurate, supplemented by a translation from the original French text where it is not. Substantial deviations from the seventeenth English translation are indicated by the use of round brackets, whereas square brackets as usual indicate editorial additions.

The original translator was often slapdash to a fault, getting numbers and basic facts wrong (muddling dates, and putting Choisy at one stage to Chaumont's right in a procession instead of on his left, and so on). In describing the attendant soldiers in the palace, the translator has them as "naked and clothed in the Moorish fashion", which is clearly contradictory. Chaumont actually wrote *pieds nus:* "barefooted, and dressed in the Moorish fashion". When the going gets difficult, the translator sometimes simply substituted a summarizing phrase, or even added one of his own. Sometimes mistranslations appear deliberate: the seventeenth century English text has Chaumont saying "to pay me all the respect which is due to the character of an Ambassador to so great a King", making it seem that Narai is the great king in question, whereas the original French has the equivalent of: "to pay me all the honours which were to due to the Ambassador of the greatest King in the World," i.e. Louis XIV. There was little love for the Sun King in England, and clearly the translator could not stomach French pretention. Many details were omitted by the translator, particularly later in the text when Chaumont lists the persons who went with him on his embassy, and, as noted, he gave up on a complete listing of the presents brought back to France. In the interests of accuracy and readability, then, the text here is modified in light of the French original; the spelling and punctuation have been modernized, but the grammar and word order have been left largely unchanged where the 1687 translation is used, and an attempt at continuity of style has been made in those passages taken from the French original and omitted in the 1687 translation. Explanatory footnotes have been kept to a minimum.

No amount of editing can overcome the fact that on occasions Chaumont is almost incoherent, notably in his description of the manner of receiving Asiatic embassies, which he clearly never witnessed and had the information second hand. On the other hand, his description of a Siamese wedding is remarkably lucid, as though he had been present himself; but one wonders if in fact he is describing a Siamese wedding or one by a Cochin-Chinese Catholic family established in Ayutthaya. Chaumont is no stylist, and the structure he adopted for his account gives rise to many repetitions.

Choisy's account of the embassy in journal form appeared in 1993 in English for the first time, but hitherto no English translation has existed of the section dealing with Siam in the eleventh volume of his *History of the*

Church, nor that, which covers almost the same ground, in his posthumous and incomplete *Memoirs towards a History of Louis XIV*. These two frequently identical accounts have been brought together here and appear as a single text in English for the first time; for convenience this has been called *Reflections on the Embassy to Siam*. The text appearing only in the *Memoirs* is indicated by broken brackets {...}, square brackets being as usual additions by the present editor. Sections appearing only in the *History of the Church* are indicated by the use of the backslash \...\. Few problems of style arise with Choisy, whose pen invariably flows smoothly (so much so that he is reputed to have said, on completing the last volume of his lengthy ecclesiastical history, that now he had finished writing it, he would have to read something about the subject).

Choisy's recollections late in life of the Siamese embassy are preceded here by two confidential memoranda, written when he was on board ship in January 1686 on the return journey to France; one deals with religious matters and the negotiations concerning the the king's possible conversion, and the other expresses Choisy's views on commerce in the Indies. Both were published in toto for the first time in 1995 (by Dirk Van der Cruysse, as Appendices III and IV to his new French edition of the Abbé's *Journal du Voyage de Siam*). Choisy's texts, lighthearted in approach but serious in content, make an admirable foil to the somewhat ponderous brevity of Chaumont, and fill in the picture of the consequences of their joint mission, firstly by describing the reception given to the Siamese ambassadors in Versailles, and finally by summarizing the events of 1688 which led to the collapse of French involvement in Siam.

*****

In the texts there is mention of *sous* or *sols*, *écus* (sometimes translated as crowns), and *pistoles*. These monetary units centred around the *livre* or pound, which, minted at Tours, in 1687 was worth 538 mg of pure gold (according to Guy Antonetti in the article on money in the *Dictionnaire du Grand Siècle*). Sixty *sous* were worth one *écu*, and one *écu* was worth three *livres*. One *pistole* was worth ten *livres*.

Taking the 1995 price of gold at US$387 per ounce, this makes the *sou* worth about 37 US cents, the *livre* approximately US$7.35, *écu* US$22.05, and the *pistole* US$73.50. The value of the gold alone (not counting the silver, screens, lacquered cabinets and masses of porcelain) in the presents brought back from Siam was thus worth, according to Choisy, US$441,000.

There is also mention of *catis* in the text. One catty was the equivalent of sixteen taels, or one and half pounds weight (0.68 kg).

*****

Bibliography

Bourges, Jacques de, *Relation du voyage de Monseigneur l'Evêque de Béryte, vicaire apostolique au Royaume de la Cochinchine, par la Turquie, la Perse, les Indes, etc., jusqu'au Royaume de Siam et autres lieux*, Paris, Bechet, 1666.

[Chaumont, Alexandre de], *Relation de l'Ambassade de Mr le Chevalier de Chaumont à la Cour du Roy de Siam*, Paris, Seneuze et Horthemels, 1686.

Choisy, Abbé François-Timoléon, *Journal du voyage de Siam fait en 1685 et 1686*, Paris, Mabre-Cramoisy, 1687 (Modern edition by Dirk Van der Cruysse, ed., Paris, Fayard, 1995; English translation by Michael Smithies, *Journal of a Voyage to Siam 1685-1686*, Kuala Lumpur, Oxford University Press, 1993).

_____, *Mémoires pour servir à l'Histoire de Louis XIV*, Utrecht (Rouen?), Van de Water (sic), 1727 (Modern edition by G. Montgrédien, ed., Paris, Mercure de France, 1983).

Gatty, J.C., *Voiage de Siam du Père Bouvet*, Leiden, Brill, 1963.

Gervaise, Nicholas, *Histoire naturelle et politique du Royaume de Siam*, Paris, Barbin, 1688 (English translation by John Villiers, *The Natural and Political History of the Kingdom of Siam*, Bangkok, White Lotus, 1989).

Hutchinson, E.W., *Adventurers in Siam in the Seventeenth Century*, London, Royal Asiatic Society, 1940; reprinted Bangkok, DD Books, 1985.

_____, *1688 Revolution in Siam: The Memoir of Father de Bèze, S.J.*, Hong Kong, University Press, 1968.

Jacq-Hergoualc'h, Michel, *Etude historique et critique du 'Journal du Voyage de Siam de Claude Céberet', Envoyé extraordinaire du Roi en 1687 et 1688*, Paris, l'Harmattan, 1992.

La Loubère, Simon de, *Du Royaume de Siam*, Paris, Coignard, 1691 (Modern edition by Michel Jacq-Hergoualc'h, ed., Paris, Editions Recherche sur les Civilisations, 1987; English translation, A *New Historical Relation of the Kingdom of Siam*, London, Horne, Saunders and Bennet, 1693, modern editions Singapore, Oxford University Press, 1986, and Bangkok, White Lotus, 1986).

Lanier, Lucien, *Etude historique sur les relations de la France et du Royaume de Siam de 1662 à 1703*, Versailles, Aubert, 1883 (Modern edition Farnborough, Gregg International, 1969).

Smithies, Michael, *The Discourses at Versailles of the first Siamese Ambassadors to France 1686-7, together with the List of their Presents to the Court*, Bangkok, The Siam Society, 1986.

_____, *The Siamese Memoirs of Count Claude de Forbin, 1685-1688*, Chiang Mai, Silkworm Books, 1997.

Tachard, Guy, *Voyage au Siam des Pères Jésuites envoyés par le Roi aux Indes et à la Chine*, Paris, Seneuze et Horthemels, 1686 and Amsterdam, Mortier, 1687 (English edition *Relation of the Voyage to Siam performed by Six Jesuits...*, London, Churchil, 1688; modern edition Bangkok, White Orchid, 1981).

_____, *Second voyage du Père Tachard et des Jésuites envoyés par le Roi au Royaume de Siam*, Paris, Horethemels, 1689, and Amsterdam, Mortier, 1689.

Van der Cruysse, Dirk, *Louis XIV et le Siam*, Paris, Fayard, 1991.

A pilot's dilemma on the journey to Siam

A RELATION OF THE EMBASSY OF MONSIEUR DE CHAUMONT, KNIGHT, TO THE COURT OF THE KING OF SIAM, WITH AN ACCOUNT OF WHATEVER PASSED THAT WAS REMARKABLE ON THE VOYAGE

PART I

Ayutthaya, capital of Siam

CHAPTER ONE

From Brest to Siam, via the Cape and Batavia[1]

I departed from Brest the 3rd of March, 1685, on the king's vessel, called the *Oiseau*,[2] accompanied by one of His Majesty's frigates, named the *Maligne*,[3] and that with so favourable a wind that in seven days we arrived opposite the Island of Madeira: we thus happily passed on till we came to four or five degrees northward of the equinoctial line, when we were overtaken by a calm, and suffered rather extreme heats, but which yet did not much incommode us. The wind began again to blow, and we passed the Line 350 degrees 5 minutes of longitude, thirty-three days after our setting out. We found the water (at the bottom of our hold) here to be as fresh and good as if it had been drawn from some pleasant fountain, which made us neglect to use that in our jars. At 5 degrees southward of

---

[1] The chapter divisions and headings have been added in this edition. Passages placed inside round brackets (...) are found in the French text but not in the 1687 English translation; only significant variations have been so noted, and where the English translation has been found wanting, the French text has been given precedence.

[2] Chaumont's vessel was in fact the *'The Bird'*, not *'The Hawk'* as the 1687 English translation states.

[3] The accompanying frigate was given throughout in the 1687 translation as *Malign*, in the sense of pithy, jaunty.

the Line we found the winds very inconstant, but the heats not troublesome, and I left not off my winter garments in all this passage.

The winds, though variable, yet carried us [on] our course, so that we arrived at the Cape of Good Hope the 31st of May, to take in fresh water, and other provisions, although my old store was still sufficient (for more than forty days. What was rather surprising was that wanting to know of the pilots how far they thought themselves from the Cape, one of them, whose face did not appear to demonstrate excessive ability, positively assured me that we would see it in two hours, as if he had seen it then, which after a navigation of more than two thousand leagues[1] without seeing land, arrived exactly as he had predicted.)

We cast anchor very late at night, and found in this road four Dutch vessels (one of which flew the colours on the mainmast) that came from Holland, and had on board a commissioner of the [Dutch] East India Company (which makes that state so powerful in the Indies), who was going there to order affairs (in the outposts belonging to the republic). Major-General de Saint Martin, a Frenchman,[2] who has been in the Dutch service this thirty years, (and with whom they are very happy,) was also in one of these vessels, intending for Batavia, where his employment lay. The commissioner-general[3] sent to compliment me the first

1   A league was a variable measure of distance, about 4 km in modern reckoning.
2   Isaac de l'Ostal de Saint-Martin (1629?-1696) came from a Béarnais family and was already working as a lieutenant for the Dutch in Batavia in 1662. Like van Reede (infra), he was a competent linguist and interested in botany and history. He was commander of the VOC's troops in the Indies, according to Choisy, Chaumont's co-ambassador.
3   Jonker Hendrik Adriaan van Reede tot Drakestein (1626-1691); he was posted in 1686 to Ceylon and the Coromandel coast.

day of my arrival; and the next morning his nephew and secretary came to offer me whatsoever I might want. The inhabitants of the country (following his order) brought presents of fruits, vegetables, and sheep, and he caused me to be saluted by these four Dutch vessels. (I could not have received more courtesy from the Dutch gentlemen in that place.)

The Dutch have in this place a small fort (with five bastions), and near an hundred houses about a musket shot off it, which are well built, and in good order (both within and without, as those in Holland. Most of the inhabitants are Catholics, although they are not free to exercise their religion). The situation of this place is very pleasant, although bounded by a great mountain, inhabited by an infinite number of huge monkeys, which oft come down even into their gardens, and eat the fruit. There are also several summer houses, two, three and four leagues off in the country; and beyond this vast mountain there is a plain near ten leagues long, where are several houses well inhabited, and which are every day increasing. The climate is mild enough, their spring beginning in October, and ending in December. Their summer lasts January, February and March, their autumn is April, May, June, and their winter in July, August, [and] September. The heats would be very great were they not moderated by the wind. The Dutch East India Company have here a most pleasant garden (with fine palisades of a wood which is always green and) whose great walk is fourteen hundred paces long; it is planted almost everywhere thick with citron trees.[1] This garden is ordered into compartments; in one of them you may see fruit trees, and the rarest plants of Asia, in the other the most exquisite of Africa, in the third such as are choicest in Europe, and in the fourth such fruits and

---

[1] Lemons.

plants as grow in America. This garden is very well kept, and of good use to the Dutch, by the great quantity of herbs and vegetables it supplies them with for the refreshment of their fleets, when they come here to pass to the Indies, or returning to their own country.

I found there a French gardener, who had heretofore learnt his trade at the gardens of Monsieur[1] at St Cloud.[2] The soil is very good, and yields (a lot of wheat and a) good store of all kinds of grain. A person worthy [of] credit has assured me he saw an hundred and sixty ears of corn on one stalk.

The inhabitants of the country have a fine physiognomy, but herein deceitful, for they are mere brutes; they go naked, excepting that part which they cover with a nasty skin of a beast. They till not the ground, yet abound with cattle, such as cows, bulls, hogs, and sheep. They scarce eat any of these, their chiefest diet being milk and butter, which they make in sheep skins. They have a root which hath the taste of our hazelnuts, which serves them for bread.[3] They are well supplied in a knowledge of simples,[4] which they can use in the cure of their wounds and other distempers. The greatest lords amongst them are they that have most cattle, which they watch and keep themselves. They oft have wars with each other about their pastures. They are greatly annoyed with wild beasts, there being more than a few lions, leopards, tigers, wolves, wild dogs, elks, and elephants. (All these animals wage war against them and their cattle.) All their arms are a kind of poisoned lance, to strike these beasts with (and kill them once they are

---

[1] Louis XIV's only brother, Philippe d'Orleans (1640-1701).
[2] Between Paris and Versailles; the Siamese ambassadors to France in 1686-7 visited and greatly admired these gardens.
[3] Presumably mealie, or maize.
[4] Remedies.

wounded). They have a kind of toils[1] wherewith they enclose their cattle at night. They trouble not themselves much about religion, yet observe some slight ceremonies to the full moon, which do not signify much. Their language is very difficult to learn. They have very much game, [such] as pheasants, partridges—three or four sorts—peacocks, hares, conies,[2] (roe-deer, deer, and boars); the deer [are] in such abundance that sometimes a man shall see near twenty thousand together in a plain. (This is what people worthy of credit have assured me.) We ate some of this game before mentioned, and found it admirably good. The sheep are here very large, of fourscore pound weight commonly. Here are [a] great quantity of cows and oxen. Many wild horses are found here, which (are the most beautiful in the world, and are striped white and black). I brought along with me one of their skins. They are hard to be mastered.

The sea in this bay is full of fish, which are of good relish, some of them having the taste of salmon (both solid and big). This place abounds with sea wolves,[3] and when in our chaloupe[4] we perceived an infinite number came tumbling by us (in front of our poop; we fired on them), of which we could not kill one.

This being such a good country, the Hollanders send continually fresh people to it, who make every season considerable discoveries. Some say they have found out gold and silver mines, of which 'tis not to be expected they should say much themselves. The water is here very good, proceeding from several springs, near rivers which abound with fish.

---

[1]   Snares or corrals.
[2]   Rabbits.
[3]   Seals.
[4]   Longboat or launch, spelt 'shallop' in the 1687 translation.

We departed from this road the 7th of June, with so favourable a north and north-north-west wind, that we soon got into the open sea, and that night steered to Bantam.[1] We endured vehement rains, and met with great seas till we reached (opposite the north and south) isles of Madagascar,[2] which was on the 19th of June. On these seas you perceive [a] great quantity of birds, but find therein no fish. Till (the 20th of) July we encountered with very boisterous seas, and met with most variable winds, which forced us 40 degrees southward, where we found a westerly wind, with which we made great way. The 24th the frigate *Maligne* was separated from us by bad weather, being driven to the north (by very heavy seas).

The 3rd of August we found the sea less troublesome, and the weather more favourable, and at break of day discovered an island seven or eight leagues before us which surprised us, it not being described in our charts.[3] It is situated 10 degrees 19 minutes of latitude southward, (and was estimated to be 120 degrees 41 minutes in longitude). This isle lies convenient for the finding of the isle of Java, which cannot be distant from it above an hundred and fifty leagues, and since we understood 'tis called the isle of Mony,[4] being ill set down in our maps, which place it near that of Java. We coasted yet two days with a fairly good wind, and on the 5th about eight in the morning we discovered the isle of Java, which gave us much joy (to find ourselves beneath the wind of the Strait of Sunda; we came with a down wind coasting along the island), and the 7th

1   Now Banten, in West Java, close to the Sunda Strait.
2   No one else makes mention of Madagascar on this well-documented voyage, though Choisy does say, on 9 June, that in two days the ship should be level with this island, though 400 leagues from it. It is not clear why Chaumont specified two islands, north and south Madagascar.
3   It was, thinks Choisy, the Cocos Islands.
4   Christmas Island, sometimes called Monin, Mony or Money.

following we found ourselves between the Prince's Isle,[1] and that of the Emperor,[2] which make the entrance of the straits.[3] The isle of the Emperor lies on the side of the island of Sumatra, and the isle of the Prince on the side of Java. We lay four days between these two islands, the winds and currents opposing us in so violent a manner that what we gained in twelve hours, we lost in four, by means of calms, which often happened.

Before we entered this strait, the frigate which lost us on the 24th of June came up to our ship-side this day[4] before we knew who she was. The 13th we left these islands behind us, and cast anchor within a league of Java. There came on board us several persons in little boats, who brought us the country's fruits, such as coco[nuts]s, the water which is contained in them being excellent drink, also melons, citrons, and several other like refreshments, which did much good to our crew, tired with the fatigues of the sea, and overrun with the scurvy.

On the 16th in the morning we came to Bantam, where I found the frigate *Maligne*, which tarried for me two days. The captain of it came and told me that the Dutch governor of the place would not give him entrance, but only presented him with some fowl and fruits; whereupon I sent Mr de Forbin,[5] my lieutenant, to compliment this governor

---

[1]   Pulau Panaitan.
[2]   Emperor Island appears to be Pulau Tabuan, close to the coast of Sumatra. It is marked in Placide's map of 1686.
[3]   The Sunda Strait, between Java and Sumatra.
[4]   It was, in fact, after they passed through the strait that they met the *Maligne*, when a ship was spotted on 15 August, but it was not confirmed as being the *Maligne* until the following day.
[5]   The impetuous Claude de Forbin (1656-1733) had already seen several years' military and naval service when he was asked to join the embassy at the age of twenty-nine. He was to stay in Siam one year, and returned to give Louis XIV a more balanced account of the country's advantages than Chaumont, Choisy, or Tachard.

from me, and entreat him to grant me leave to land my sick men, to take in fresh water, and other necessaries. He returned answer that he was not master of Bantam, (that he was but as the leader of the auxiliary troops,) and that it was the King of Bantam who commanded, who would not admit any stranger to his country. The Hollanders made use of this king's name, being unwilling that foreign vessels should come amongst them, especially those from Europe. Since they have settled there, they have driven all other nations out.[1]

'Tis a great town, and well peopled by the natives. Before the Hollanders became masters of it, 'twas the chiefest place of the Indies for commerce; people came there from Europe, Persia, China, Japan, the Great Mogul's empire,[2] and divers other parts (in the Indies), but now the Hollanders have got all commerce into their hands, which is of vast advantage to them; for this place may be compared to what heretofore was Cadiz[3] in Spain.

As soon as I received the governor's answer, who yet told me that if I would go to Batavia, I should find there a kind reception, I therefore weighed anchor, and set sail for that place, to which there's but fifteen leagues. I was three days before I arrived there; for having no pilot that was acquainted with those parts, I fell on several islands and shallows, which caused me to cast anchor every night, and in the daytime to move with small sail, sounding all places I went over: but I arrived on the 18th at night, where as soon as I had cast anchor, I sent Mr de Forbin to the [governor-] general[4] to compliment him, and to desire leave to bring

---

[1]   Both Choisy and Forbin give a much more detailed account of the Dutch intrigues in Bantam.

[2]   Aurangzeb (r. 1658-1707)

[3]   The English text spelles this Cales, the French text, Cadix.

[4]   Johannes Camphuys (1634-1695) started his career as a goldsmith's

my sick men on shore, and take in (water and) refreshments. He took my compliment in good part, and returned answer he would give orders for all that was necessary for me. I sent next morning sixty-five sick men on shore, who all recovered their healths in seven days that I tarried at Batavia (through the good treatment and the refreshments I had made available). On the 19th in the morning the [governor-]general sent me a compliment by three officers (with the offer of all that I might need), and desired me to come on shore (to relieve me of the fatigues of the sea), offering me his own house of which I would be the master. After necessary thanks, I answered that I wished my orders (which prevented me from landing) would have permitted me that liberty (and without that I would have accepted with joy such courtesy. I replied in such a manner, apart from many other reasons, to avoid the ceremonies which would have been necessary on such an occasion). The general sent me a great chaloupe laden with all sorts of Indian fruits, herbs, new bread, two oxen, two sheep, and thus continued every two days presenting us.

On the 28th I landed incognito, and viewed the town in a small boat. 'Tis like Venice, having canals which run through every street, and planted with great trees which yield an agreeable shade, as well to the canals as the streets. The houses are built as they are in Holland (and with the same cleanliness). There is a citadel (with four bastions). The town is enclosed with a wall, and a great ditch, but not deep. The surroundings are very fine, with country houses round about with very handsome gardens and fish-ponds, wherein are admirable fish of all sorts (and many colours; I saw many both silver and gold). In this town are many

apprentice in Holland and came to Batavia in 1654. He rose through all the company's ranks, and was made Governor-General in August 1685.

exceedingly rich traders, who spare no cost for their delight; (their freedom is the same as in Holland, particularly in regard to women). I spoke with four or five of them in my walks in the gardens; their dresses are like the French.[1] There is in Batavia about fifty coaches, some of which are very stately (and in the French manner): their horses are not of the biggest, but to make amends, are very lively. This town is a place of vast commerce, and its riches are so great that the inhabitants need not be sparing of their gold and silver. 'Tis extraordinarily well peopled, and the Dutch keep a strong garrison; they have there near three thousand Moors[2] (from the coast of Malabar) who are slaves, and several of the natives they keep under their obedience, who live about the town.

The isle of Java, on which this city is situated, is very populous, and comprises two hundred leagues in length, and forty in breadth. It has five kings,[3] over whom the Hollanders are masters; all these people are Mohammedans. I sent to the [governor-]general for a pilot for Siam, mine having never been there; he lent me one who had sailed there four times; for all these civilities, I sent Mr de Forbin to thank him.

On Sunday, being the 26th of August, at six of the clock in the morning, we set sail, and steered our course to pass the Strait of Bangka; we advanced that day ten leagues with a small wind, and at nine at night I was told of a sail that

---

[1] The 1687 English translation "neither do they deny themselves unlawful satisfaction with women. I took the liberty myself to entertain four or five at divers times in my walks in the gardens" makes it appear Chaumont accosted prostitutes, which the French text makes perfectly clear was not the case.

[2] The term 'Moors' was, as can be seen, used very loosely; often it meant no more than 'Muslims'.

[3] Chaumont's five kingdoms were probably Mataram, Madura, Surabaya, Cirebon and Bantam.

made towards my vessel, whereupon I bid the officer be prepared; when immediately I saw out of my window this ship coming up to us. We called out to know what she was, but could have no answer, and coming on the deck, I found all our men under arms, and the bowsprit of this ship laid on cross my stern. I caused about twenty musket shot to be fired among her, which immediately made her clear herself of us, and clapped on all her sails. We knew not what nation she was of, for nobody in the ship spoke a word, and we observed but few men on board her. I suppose her to have been some merchant ship, guided by unskilful lands; they did our ship some mischief (to the taffrail), but the damage was repaired next morning.[1]

On Tuesday, being the 28th, at night we discovered the entrance to the Strait of Bangka, and on the 29th in the morning we entered therein. Although we had a good Dutch pilot, yet we ran upon a muddy bank of sand, there being many of this kind in this strait, and it being usual for vessels to meet with them without much hurt; therefore this did not much disturb us. (I caused a small anchor to be let down on the Sumatran side) and in less than two hours we got off clear from this bank. We were four days passing this strait.

The isle of Sumatra is on the left and extends two hundred and fifty leagues in length, and about fifty in breadth. The Hollanders have four or five fortresses here, its people are Mohammedans, and under the regiment of four or five kings. The Queen of Aceh possesses one of the largest countries, and governs with great authority and regularity. The Hollanders are in a manner masters of all these princes; they deal with them for whatsoever the island yields, where 'tis said there are gold mines, much

---

[1] The ship was the Dutch vessal *Berquemeer* and it collided with the *Oiseau* through pilot's negligence.

pepper, quantities of rice, all sorts of cattle, and in some cantons the people are very barbarous, and the kings are oft at war with one another. Those who receive the Hollanders' protection are ever the strongest (because of the troops and vessels these people send them): 'Tis the same in the isle of Java, for three hundred Europeans do beat five or six thousand men of these nations, who know not the art of war. It lies 4 degrees southward of the equinoctial line. The Dutch have a fort on the side of the Strait of Bangka, strengthened with twenty-four cannons; the fort is built upon a great river called Palembang,[1] which runs so violently into the sea that three or four months in the year, in rainy weather, the water of it when in the sea does yet keep its freshness.

The isle of Bangka lay on the right hand of us, being about forty leagues long. The Dutch have a fort there, and trade with the natives of the island: 'tis said to be a very good and fruitful country. When I sailed by the River of Palembang, the Dutch were there lading two vessels with pepper. On the 3rd of September we passed the Line again in the best of weather, the most favourable we could have hoped for, and without excessive heats, with a temperate air (and not hotter than this same month in France), so that I still wore my cloth suit, which I had donned by the coasts of Africa. We came before the Strait of Malacca, which has three or four passages, or entrances, but the currents were so great, and running sometimes for us and sometimes against us, that we were forced oft to cast anchor; for when the calm took us, the currents forcibly carried us a great distance; but we left not this coast, by reason of the winds, which always blow from the land, and greatly helped us in our course. I believe this country's air to be good, for we had many sick, who were all recovered by it.

[1]   Actually called the Musi.

On the 5th we discovered the isle of Poltimon,[1] which is inhabited by Malays, who are Mohammedans. This is plentiful land, and obedient to a prince by whom 'tis governed. The Queen of Aceh has some pretentions to it, and for this effect she sends thither every year some vessels; but this prince being not willing to engage in a war against her, this people pay her tribute. There came a small boat to our ship's side, which brought us some fish and fruits. This isle is distant from the continent about six leagues, and part of its coasts was heretofore subject to the King of Siam; but it has been since some years in the possession of two or three kings, one of which is the King of the Malays. This is a very unsociable nation, and will enter into no commerce.

From the 5th to the 15th we had but small winds, and very variable, and calms which caused us oft to cast anchor, as also by reason of currents which run along this coast. From the Strait of Bangka to Siam, the land is not wont to be left, (and one only moves between fifteen and twenty fathoms of muddy bottom).

The same day we found ourselves before Ligor,[2] which is the chief place belonging to the King of Siam (on this coast). The Hollanders have a habitation there, and liberty of trade. 'Tis hard to express the joy which the Siamese whom we brought along with us had to see the lands of their king,[3] and it cannot be better compared than to that which we felt at our return, when God brought us safe to Brest. Here died a young gentleman (named d'Herbouville,

---

[1] Pulao Tioman, 'Poltimont', to the east of Malaya.

[2] Ligor was the name usually given by foreigners to what is now Nakhon Si Thammarat.

[3] The two envoys returning to Siam from France, Khun Pichai Walit and Khun Pichit Maitri, were considered uncouth and uncomely, which is why Chaumont later refers to the attendant Siamese nobles as 'well-shaped' and showing signs of distinction.

one of the marine guards), having been ill five months with a bloody flux, whom the king sent to attend me in my voyage; he was a youth of great hopes, and I was much afflicted at the loss of him[1].

---

[1]   Chaumont was wrong. The embassy arrived off Ligor on 15 September as he states, but the Chevalier d'Herbouville, who had been sick since leaving Batavia, died on 6 September. Tachard notes "Le sixième Septembre Monsieur Devandcrets d'Herbouville Gentilhomme de la suite de Monsieur l'Ambassadeur, mourut dans la Frégate en la fleur de son âge" (Amsterdam 1688: 138). Father Bouvet and Choisy both also give this date, even if the spelling of the name varies.

CHAPTER TWO

Arrival in Siam

In short, thanks be to God, on the 24th we cast anchor before the river of Siam.[1] Our whole ship's crew and my attendants were in good health. I sent to the Bishop of Metellopolis[2] Mr Le Vachet,[3] a Missionary, who came with the mandarins[4] into France, and whom I brought along with them, with charge to entreat him to come to me that I might learn what had happened this eighteen months since the King of Siam sent [his envoys] into France.

On the 29th the bishop came on board with the Abbé de Lionne,[5] who informed me of whatsoever had passed,

[1] The Chao Phya.

[2] Louis Laneau (1637-1696), in Siam from 1664 until his death. He later warned Chaumont of King Narai's real intentions in matters of religion, and was imprisoned for two years after the coup d'état of 1688.

[3] Bénigne Vachet (1641-1720), often Le Vacher in contemporary spelling, a Missionary in Siam from 1668 to 1683. He accompanied the Siamese envoys to France as interpreter in 1684-5, and fell out of favour with the Marquis de Seignelay, Secretary of State for the Navy, for promising King Narai impossibly tall mirrors.

[4] Pichai Walit and Pichit Maitri.

[5] Artus (1655-1713), son of the Secretary of State Hugue de Lionne, and Missionary in Siam from 1681. He was an interpreter for the Siamese embassy to France 1686-7, left Siam after the events of 1688

telling me that the King of Siam having heard at midnight of my arrival by Mr Constance,[1] one of his ministers, he showed great joy, and ordered him to go and advise the bishop of it, and to dispatch two mandarins of the first rank, who are in a manner as the chief gentlemen of the king's chamber are in France, to assure me of the joy he conceived at my arrival. They came two days after on board me, whom I received in my cabin (seated in an armchair); the bishop sitting close by me (on a small seat), and they likewise, with some others (from the ship who were there) sitting down on carpets laid on the floor of my cabin, it being the custom of the country to sit in that manner, there being no person (other than those who are to be shown great distinction) who sits higher than them.

They told me the king their master had commanded them to show me the joy he had at my arrival, and at the news of our king's having vanquished all his enemies, and become absolute master of his kingdom (enjoying the peace he had brought to the whole of Europe). Having denoted to them how much I thought myself beholden to the goodness of the king their master, and answered what they offered touching our prince, I told them I was extremely satisfied with the governor of Bangkok, for his reception of those I sent him, as also with the presents he had made me. They replied he had done only his duty, seeing in France the king their master's envoys had been so well received and that

for China as Bishop of Rosalie, and returned to Paris, where he died. The English translation calls him the Abbat of Lionne, which is hardly exact.

[1] Constantine Phaulkon, or Gherakis, always referred to by the French as 'Monsieur Constance'. Of obscure Levantine origin and born in Cephalonia, he early became a cabin-boy in the English East India Company, went to the Indies, and, thanks to quick wit and genuine linguistic ability, rose rapidly to power, becoming in effect chief minister in Siam about 1683. He died after torture in the 1688 coup.

moreover I merited this good usage by my (having once caused the) procurement of an union between the kings of Siam and of France. (These are their ways of speaking which contain much floridity.) Having treated them with the honours and civilities usual in such like occasions in these countries, I presented them with tea and comfits.[1] These two mandarins were well-shaped men, of about twenty-five years of age, and apparelled after their mode, being bare-headed, without shoes or stockings, wearing a kind of long scarf (from their waist) down to their knees, without being pleated and, coming between their legs, was fastened behind, (falling like breeches with no seat). The scarf was of painted linen neatly done, (the finest in the country) and well embroidered (some four inches broad) at the edges; from the waist upwards, they had nothing but a kind of muslin waistcoat, which they let hang over this scarf, the sleeves falling to just below the elbow. They remained about an hour on board our vessel, and I saluted them with nine pieces of cannon at their departure.

On the 1st of October, Mr Constance, the King of Siam's minister I lately mentioned, and who though a stranger has obtained by his merit the chief place in the king's favour, sent to compliment me by his secretary, who was an honest man, and offered me from himself such a great present of fruits, besides oxen, hogs, pullets, ducks and such like things, that all the ships' crew were fed with them for four days together. These refreshments are most agreeable when a man has been seven months at sea.

On the 8th the Bishop of Metellopolis, who had returned to the chief city of Siam, came on board us again with mandarins to enquire as from the king after my health, and to inform me how impatiently he took my delays of seeing him, entreating me to hasten on shore. I returned their

---

[1]   Sweets.

compliment, (saying I was much affected by the continuing bounty of the king their master,) and told them I was preparing to go on shore. I gave these mandarins the same entertainment I gave the first, saluting them also at their departure with nine pieces of cannon.

About two of the clock the same day I went into my chaloupe, and those of my attendants into boats which the king had sent; being arrived at night in the river, I found five very neat barges, one for myself, which was a very magnificent one, and the four others for the gentlemen who accompanied me, with several others to carry the rest of my retinue and goods. (The barges are certain kinds of boats which I shall describe later.) Two mandarins came and complimented me from the king. I could not reach that night the place designed for my reception, which obliged me to pass out of the barge into the frigate *Maligne*, which had entered the river two days before, on board of which I lay all night.

The same evening, the purser whom I had sent to Siam to buy such provisions as we needed (for the [king's] ship and the frigate) came and told me that Mr Constance had delivered to him from the king eleven barks full of oxen, pigs, calves, ducks, pullets, and arrack or strong water made with rice, (for the provision of the crew of the two ships,) together with a request that I would not spare to ask for what we wanted, for we should be supplied all the time we tarried in the kingdom at His Majesty's charge.

On the 9th there came two mandarins to my barge from the king, who told me they came for my orders, and I parted from this place about seven in the morning. Having went about five leagues, I came to a house built on purpose for my entertainment, when two mandarins and the governors of Bangkok and Pipely[1] with several others came

[1]   Phetchaburi.

to compliment me on my arrival, and wished me a long life. This house was made with bamboos, (which is a very light wood,) and covered with neat mats. All the furniture in it was new; it contained several chambers hung with fine painted linen, the floor of my room was covered with a very fine carpet. I found there a dais with a very rich gold cloth, a gilded armchair, square cushions with fine velvet covers, a table with a covering of gold brocade, and magnificent beds. I was here served with meats and fruits in quantity. I left the place after dinner,[1] and all the mandarins followed me. I went to Bangkok, which is the chief place the King of Siam has on this river, distant about twelve leagues from the sea. I found here an English vessel, which saluted me with his twenty-one cannon, and the forts which defend both sides of the river also saluted me, (the one with twenty-nine, and the other with thirty-one salutes); these forts are regular enough and well furnished with (large cast-iron) guns. I lodged (in the fortress to the left) in a house quite well built and furnished, where I was treated after the fashion of the country.

The next morning (the 10th) I departed at eight of the clock attended by all the mandarins and governors who were come to compliment me. (Two other mandarins came to compliment me.) At my departure I was also saluted (in the same manner as the previous day) and arrived at noon in a house built on purpose for me, and as well furnished as the former.[2] There was near adjoining two fortresses which saluted me with all their guns, and two mandarins more came to receive me. I was very well served at dinner; and I departed here at three o'clock; (the forts saluted me as

---

[1]   Lunch, in today's parlance.

[2]   Forbin maintains all these houses were erected and dismantled one after the other as the party progressed up-river, and the same furnishings were shifted into them.

before,) and the governor of Bangkok took his leave of me to return to his charge. Holding on my course I came to two ships, the one English and the other Dutch, lying at anchor, who discharged all their artillery, and I arrived at seven at night at a house constructed and furnished after the same manner as the preceding ones, where I was received and very well treated by other mandarins.

The 11th in the morning I departed thence, and went and dined in another house, and at night I lay in a house made much like the others, and very well furnished, where two mandarins received me.

On the 12th I left and I lodged two leagues off [the city of] Siam, where I was received by two mandarins. The principal merchants of the English and Dutch Companies came to compliment me on my arrival in those parts, and as to the French they had come to see me on board and attended me all the way. Here I remained until I made my entrance.[1] (I noticed that all the houses that had been built for me were painted red, although only those of the king are in this colour.)

---

[1] His formal entrance into the city.

CHAPTER THREE

At the city of Siam

The river of Siam called the Menam[1] is very large and commodious; (it has everywhere at least four fathoms of water, extending to eight or nine in most parts,) being adorned all along the sides of it with pleasant trees; but three or four months in the year all these places are overflowed with water, and therefore all the houses are built on piles,[2] and made all of bamboos. This wood serves the Siamese both for the foundations, floors, and tops of their houses, and for infinite purposes besides, making use of it as we do flints and steels, for they need only take a little of this wood on a heap, and rub it together, and it presently lights.

All the people of these parts have little canals and boats to pass from one house to another for their transactions. Here are seen almost none but women to work, the men being for the most part employed in the king's service, whose slaves they are. I had the same honours showed me as to the King of Siam when he is wont to pass on the river. All people were in barges, or on the side of the river, lying

---

[1]   It was (and still is) called the Chao Phya, but all foreigners called it the Menam (which Chaumont spells Menan), meaning simply river.

[2]   The 1687 translation had 'sledges', a frame or a platform.

flat on their bellies, and their hands joined against their foreheads. (In front of the houses and the villages there was a kind of parapet raised seven or eight feet above the water, made with matting.) The Siamese reverence in such a manner their prince, that they dare not lift up their eyes to look at him.

All the mandarins which came to receive me on the river still accompanied me. (The first were like gentlemen of the chamber, and the others, who came afterwards, were always of greater consideration than those preceding them.) The princes visited me last. These mandarins have all very neat barges, in the middle of which there is a kind of throne whereon they sit, and they usually go but one in a barge, on both sides of them are their arms, as sabres, lances, swords, darts, breastplates, and even [pitch]forks. They are all clothed in the manner I already mentioned. A Portuguese whom the king had made general of the troops in Bangkok continually accompanied me, and gave orders for all things. I was attended with near fifty or sixty barges, some of which were fifty, sixty, seventy, and eighty foot long, having oars from twenty to an hundred. They row not after our manner; they sit two on each bench, one on one side and another on the other, their faces turned on that side where they go, and have a scull, which they call pagais,[1] being about four foot long, with which they take a world of pains, being content with sod rice[2] and if they have a piece of fish, they believe they dine sumptuously.

They eat of a leaf which they call betel, which is like ivy, and a kind of [a]corn which they call areca, putting lime thereon and this gives it a taste. They eat the tobacco growing in their country, which is very strong, all [of]

---

1   They did not call them this; the French word *pagaïe* simply means paddle. The Siamese is most commonly *pai*.
2   Boiled rice.

which blackens their teeth, which they esteem the handsomest. A man may live after this rate for fifteen (or twenty) *sous* a month, for the Siamese usually drink nothing but water. They have a kind of aqua vitae which they call arrack, made with rice. When I came to an house which was intended for me, all the mandarins that accompanied me (and those who received me) made a lane for me to pass through to my chamber door.

On the 13th I sent word to the king by the mandarins that were with me that I had been informed of the manner wherewith they were wont to receive ambassadors in his kingdom, and it being very different from that of France, I entreated him to send me somebody to discuss about the subject of my [formal] entrance.

On the 14th he sent me the Sieur Constance, with whom I had a long conversation, the Bishop of Metellopolis being our interpreter.[1] We had a tedious dispute, and I would [a]bate nothing of the mode of receiving ambassadors in France, which he granted me.

On the 15th the Tonkinese came to compliment me on my arrival. The 16th the Cochin-Chinese did the same.

The 17th Mr Constance came to me, and brought with him four stately barges to carry the presents which His Majesty sent to the King of Siam. (Among those presents were several pieces of brocade with a gold background and flowers the same, four very fine Savonnerie carpets, large silver chandeliers, very large mirrors decorated with gold and silver, a number of clocks and small bureaux artistically worked, several guns and small pistols, of admirable workmanship; and many other examples of French craftsmanship.) And on the same day the king gave order to all the Indian nations that reside at Siam to congratulate [me on] my arrival, and to pay me all the respect which is due

---

[1]   The medium being either Siamese or Portuguese.

to the character of an ambassador of the greatest king in the world.[1] They came to me at six at night, each of them habited after their own manner; they were of forty different nations, and each of them of kingdoms independent one of another, and that which seemed most remarkable was that among the rest there was the son of a king who was driven out of his country, and taking Siam for his refuge, entreated assistance toward his re-establishment.[2] Their dresses were almost the same as those of the Siamese, except for some having turbans, others Armenian bonnets, others skull-caps, and others bare-headed, like the common Siamese, persons of quality having bonnets of the same fashion as our dragoons which stand upright, made of white muslin which tie under their chins with a string, being all of them barefooted (except for a few who wore babouches like those worn by the Turks).

The king had Mr Constance tell me that he would give me audience the next morning, being the 18th. I set out at seven of the clock in the morning in the manner which I shall relate, having first recited the honour wherewith the King of Siam received the King of France's letter. 'Tis true he is wont to receive with respect the letters delivered him by ambassadors of foreign potentates, but he would (in justice) give a distinct honour to that of our great monarch. There came forty of the chiefest mandarins in the court, two of which were *oyas*, which is to say like dukes in France, who told me that all the barges were ready to receive His Majesty's letter, and carry myself to the palace. The letter was in my chamber in a golden receptacle (covered with a

---

[1]   One suspects the 1687 mistranslation here, "to pay me all the respect which is due to the character of an ambassador to so great a king", is wilful.

[2]   This may be one of the Makassar princes, driven out by the Dutch, and who was to cause such trouble soon after.

very rich brocade drape). The mandarins having entered, prostrated themselves, their hands closed and adjoining to their foreheads, and their faces towards the ground, and saluted in this posture the king's letter for three times together, I being seated on an armchair near the letter; this honour was never paid to any but His Majesty of France. Which ceremony being ended, I took the letter with the golden receptacle, and having carried it seven or eight paces, I gave it to the Abbé de Choisy,[1] who came from France with me. He walked at my left hand a little behind, and carried it to the waterside, where I found a very handsome barge, sumptuously gilded, in which were two mandarins of the chief rank. I took the letter from the Abbé de Choisy, and having carried it into the barge with me, I put it into the hands of one of these mandarins, who laid it on a very high entirely gilded tapering dais. After that I entered another [barge], which immediately followed that wherein was the letter of His Majesty. Two others also as stately as mine, in which were mandarins, rowed on either side of that where the letter was. Mine, as I now said, followed after. The Abbé de Choisy was in another barge immediately behind, and the gentlemen which accompanied me, and others of my retinue were in other barges. Those of the great mandarins likewise were very fine, and were on head of us. There were about twelve gilt barges, and near two hundred others (which formed two columns). The king's letter, the two barges that attended it, and mine, were in the middle. All the nations at Siam were attending, and the whole river, although very broad, was covered with barges. We moved after this rate to the town, whose cannons saluted me, which never was done to any other

---

[1] Given as the 'Abbat of Choisy' in the 1687 translation. This is the first mention of Chaumont's co-ambassador, which appears to indicate the measure the author had of his colleague.

ambassador, all the ships in the port did likewise, and on landing, I found a great golden chariot in which only the king rode.

I took His Majesty's letter, and laid it into this chariot, which was drawn by horses and pushed by men. I afterwards went into a gilded chair, which was carried by ten men on their shoulders; the Abbé de Choisy was also in another, but of less finery; the gentlemen and mandarins which accompanied me were on horseback, [and] all the several nations which dwell in Siam walking on foot behind. The procession was in this wise to the castle (of the governor)[1] where I found the soldiers who were drawn up on each side of the street, having headpieces of gilt metal, red shirts, and a kind of scarf of painted cloth, which served them for breeches, but having neither shoes nor stockings. Some of them were armed with muskets, others with lances, others with bows and arrows, and lastly some with pikes.

There wanted not musical instruments, as trumpets, drums, timbrels, pipes, little bells, and horns (which music sounded like that of shepherds in France). All this music made a deal of noise; and thus marched we the length of a great street, through an infinite number of people (on both sides, and all the squares were likewise filled). We came at length to a great open place, in front of which stood the king's palace, where were ranged on each side elephants of war. We afterwards entered into the first court of the palace, where I saw about two thousand soldiers seated on their backsides, with the butt-end of their muskets to the ground standing upright; they were placed six in a rank, in a direct line (and dressed as I have indicated). There were

---

[1]   This appears not to be the royal palace; it might have been the Wang Na, the Front Palace, but seems more likely to have been in the area of Phaulkon's compound on the south-east corner of the city.

on the left several armed elephants, ready for war. We afterwards saw an hundred men on horseback, barefooted, and clothed after the Moorish fashion, having a lance in their hands. In this place those of foreign nations left me, excepting some gentlemen who accompanied me all the way. I passed into two other courts, which were garrisoned after the same manner, and I entered into another, where was a great number of mandarins, all of them prostrate on the ground. Here were six horses held, each of them by two mandarins; they had golden rings on their front hoofs, were well harnessed, (all their bridles, breast straps, cruppers, stirrup straps) being of gold and silver, covered with pearls, rubies and diamonds so thick that a man could scarce see the leather; their stirrups and saddles were of gold and silver. There were also several elephants harnessed in the same manner the coach horses were, (having crimson velvet-covered harnesses with golden clasps).

The gentlemen entered into the hall of audience, and placed themselves before the king came into his throne, and when I entered, attended by Mr Constance, the Barcalon[1] and the Abbé de Choisy who carried the king's letter, I was surprised to see the king on a most high throne, for Mr Constance had agreed with me that the king should be on a throne in his tribune no higher than a man, and that I might give my letter with my own hand. Then I told the Abbé de Choisy the promise they made me was forgotten but that I would not give the king's letter but to my height. The golden receptacle[2] wherein 'twas put had a great gold

---

[1] Barcalon was a Portuguese corruption of *Phra Klang*, the minister for foreign affairs and trade, and usually by foreigners assumed to be the chief minister. At the time the Barcalon was Okya Phra Sedet, a person with little power beside Phaulkon.

[2] In the illustration provided by La Loubère, the receptacle resembled a chalice, which is perhaps more exact than the dish shown in the famous print of this moment.

handle, more than three foot long. 'Twas imagined I would take hold of the receptacle by the end of the handle, thus to raise it to the king's throne, but I made my decision to present His Majesty's letter to the king (holding in my hand the golden cup in which it was placed). Being then come to the door, I saluted the king, the like I did also in the midway, and when I was near the place where I was to sit; having uttered two words of my harangue, I put my hat on, and sat down, and continued my discourse in these terms:

HARANGUE OF THE CHEVALIER DE CHAUMONT TO THE KING OF SIAM

Sire:

The king my master, who is now so famous in the world by his great victories and the peace he has often granted his enemies at the head of his armies, has commanded me to come to Your Majesty, to assure you of the particular esteem he has of you.

He knows, Sire, your princely qualities, the wisdom of your government, the magnificence of your court, the grandeur of your states, and especially the goodwill you bear his person, demonstrated by your ambassadors and confirmed by the continual protection you show his subjects, especially to the bishops (who are ministers of the true God).

He experiences so many marks of kindness from you as makes him ready (to respond with all that is in his power; in this design he is ready) to keep a continual correspondence with you, to (send you his subjects to undertake and) increase commerce with you, (to provide you with all the signs of a sincere friendship), but especially to begin an union between these two crowns, which will be the more famous to posterity, by your country's lying so distant from his [and] the vast seas which separate them.

But nothing will so much keep him in this resolution, and more unite him to you, than to live together in the opinions of the same belief.

And this is, Sire, what the king my master, who is so wise and enlightened a prince, and who has never failed in his advice to the kings his allies, has especially enjoined me to recommended to you.

He conjures you, as the sincerest of your friends, and by the interest which he already has in your (true glory), to consider that this supreme majesty with which you are endued[1] on earth can come only from the true God, that is to say, from a Being almighty, eternal and infinite, such as the Christians acknowledge Him to be, by whom alone kings reign, (and who regulates the fate of all peoples). Submit your greatness to this God, who governs heaven and earth: this is what's far more reasonable (than to submit to other divinities which are adored in the Orient) and of whose insignificancy Your Majesty's great judgment and penetration cannot choose but be sensible.

But Your Majesty will more clearly perceive this if you would be pleased to hear at some length the bishops and the Missionaries[2] who are here.

The best news, Sire, I can carry to the king my master is that Your Majesty, being convinced of the truth, has taken instruction into the Christian religion. (This will give him greater admiration and esteem for Your Majesty, it will stimulate his subjects to come with greater celerity and confidence into your realm, and it will succeed in bringing the glory of Your Majesty to its highest peak, since by this means it assures your person eternal happiness in heaven, after having reigned with so much prosperity on earth.)

---

[1] Invested.

[2] These are the French missionaries, sent by the Société des Missions Etrangères (founded in Paris in 1659), of whom the Bishop of Metellopolis was head in Siam.

This harangue was interpreted by Mr Constance.[1] I afterwards told His Majesty that the king my master had given me the Abbé de Choisy, and those twelve gentlemen for my company, whom I presented to him. I took the letter from the hands of the Abbé de Choisy, and carried it in the design of presenting it, no otherwise than I before mentioned. Mr Constance, who accompanied me, crawling on his hands and knees, called out to me, and making signs I should stretch out my arm up to the king, I made as if I understood not what he told me, (and stayed steadfast), when the king, smiling, arose, and stooped down to take the letter out of the cup, and that in such a manner as one might see his whole body. As soon as he had taken it, I made my obeisance and retired to my seat. The king enquired of news of His Majesty, and all the royal family, and whether the king had made any conquest of late. I told him he had gained Luxemburg, an almost impregnable place, and the most considerable the Spaniards[2] held in that country, which shut up the frontiers of France, and opened a way to those who might become his enemies, and that he had lately agreed to a peace with all Europe[3] when at the head of his armies.

The king replied he was glad of our king's great victories over his enemies, and the peace he enjoyed; he added he had sent ambassadors to France, who embarked

---

[1]   More or less; he omitted all the contentious parts concerning religion, which did not escape the Bishop of Metellopolis, who was present throughout the audience and who understood both standard Thai and the royal language *rajasap* used for addressing the king, as Chaumont makes clear below.

[2]   Luxemburg was Spanish from 1506 to 1684 and again from 1698 to 1714.

[3]   Probably a reference to the treaties of Nijmegen 1678 and 1679 between France, the United Provinces, Spain, Sweden, and the Holy Roman Empire.

at Bantam, in the *Soleil d'Orient*;[1] that he would seek all ways to give the king satisfaction in everything I proposed to him. The Bishop of Metellopolis was present, who interpreted several questions the king made me.

This monarch had a crown enriched with diamonds, fastened on a cap, which stood above the crown almost like our dragoons, his vest was of a very rich flowered stuff, wrought with gold, and embroidered at the neck and sleeves with diamonds, which looked like a kind of collar and bracelets. He had a great many diamond rings on his fingers; I cannot say what kind of shoes or stockings he had on, having only in this audience seen half his body.

The king is about fifty-five years of age,[2] well shaped, somewhat tanned as all of those countries are, having a cheerful countenance. His inclinations are royal, he is courageous, a great politician, governing alone, magnificent, liberal, a lover of arts, in a word, a prince, who (by the strength of his genius) has freed himself from diverse customs which he found in his kingdom, borrowing of foreign countries, and especially of Europe whatsover he thought might most contribute to the honour and happiness of his reign.

Throughout this audience he had four score mandarins in his hall where I was, all prostrate on the ground, and who never left this posture all this while. They had neither shoes nor stockings, and were apparelled like those I have heretofore spoke of; each of them had a box, wherein he put

---

[1] *The Soleil d'Orient* (given in the 1687 translation as 'The Rising Sun') left Bantam in 1681 with Siamese ambassadors on board and numerous presents for Louis XIV and his court. It sank, presumably in a storm, off Madagascar at the end of the year. The two envoys accompanied by Vachet were sent in 1664 to enquire the fate of the missing mission, though King Narai had already been informed of this by Louis Laneau, Bishop of Metellopolis.

[2] Narai was born about 1632, making him around fifty-three in 1685.

his betel, areca, lime and tobacco. By these boxes a man may distinguish their qualities and ranks, some differing from other. After the king had discoursed with me an hour, he shut his window, and I retired.

The place of audience was about twelve or fifteen steps high, 'twas finely painted within with big flowers of gold, from the top to the bottom, the ceiling had gilded bosses, and the floor was covered with rich carpets. At the end of the parlour there were two pairs of large stairs on each hand, which led onto the chamber where the king was; in the middle of these two pair of stairs is a folding window, before which there were three great umbrellas, tiered from the bottom of the chamber to the top; they were of cloth of gold, and their sticks covered with gold leaf; one was in the middle of the window, and the two others on both sides. 'Tis through this window we saw the king's throne, and through which he gave me audience.

Mr Constance carried me afterwards to view the rest of the palace. There, I saw the white elephant, who ate and drank out of gold. I saw also others, very fine ones, after which I returned to my lodging in the same pomp wherein I came; which house was good enough, and all my retinue was well accommodated in it. I was informed that Mr Constance had given order from the king to all the mandarins of foreign nations that dwell in his kingdom to come to these lodgings (which he had caused to be prepared for the ambassador of France) and, being there, he told them the king was minded they should see in what distinct manner he treated the ambassador of France and those from kings of other nations, this distinction being due to the King of France, a most mighty monarch, and who knew to requite the civilities showed him. These mandarins were astonished and answered they had never seen an ambassador from France and were persuaded that the singular reception which the king gave him was due to the character of so great and powerful a prince as is the King of France, seeing his victories have long since been known to the remotest part of the world; and therefore they were not surprised at the king's distinction (between this ambassador and those of his neighbouring kings). At the same time, Mr Constance ordered them from the king to come and compliment me (as I have already said).

The same day at night Mr Constance came again to see me, and then we had a longer conversation. There were in my lodgings a great number of mandarins and Siamese as a guard, and to furnish us what things we needed, at the king's charge.

On the 19th there came a great many mandarins to attend me, and Mr Constance sent me presents of fruits, and of that country's sweetmeats. The same day the Bishop of Metellopolis was sent for by the king to interpret His Majesty's letter.

On the 22nd the king sent me several pieces of brocade, morning gowns of Japan, and a set of gold buttons, and to the gentlemen which accompanied me some stuffs of gold, silver, Indian work, the king's custom being to present at one's arrival stuffs wherewith to make clothes after the fashion of the country. But as for my part I made no new clothes, and there were only the gentlemen of my train who did it. At night, being accompanied by the bishop, I went to give a visit to Mr Constance.

On the 24th the king informed me through him that he would grant me audience the following morning. The 25th I came to the palace with all my train, together with the bishop. The king gave me particular audience, wherein he told me many things, of which I gave an account to His Majesty. I dined in the palace garden under great trees and I was served with several dishes of meat and fruits (in different services; the forks and spoons for me were of gold, and those presented to the gentlemen who accompanied me and other persons who ate with me were of silver). The chief mandarins of the king as [well as] the great treasurers, the captains of the king's guards, and others attended us. This treat held three or four hours. There was in the garden a pond, in which there were a great many very rare fish, and amongst others there was one which represented the countenance of a man.[1]

On the 29th I went to give a visit to the Barcalon, who is the king's chief minister, who seemed to me to be a man of sense. The bishop accompanied me, and interpreted what I said to him.

On the 30th I went to the palace to see the pagoda of the King of Siam's domestic temple. There was in the court of the palace a combat, or to speak better, a kind of elephant fight, for the elephants were tied by the two hind legs. On each of them rode two men, who held in their hands a crook with which they governed them, as horses are managed by a bridle. They struck them several times with it to animate them, and the elephants had fought well no question, had they had liberty; they only gave one another blows with their teeth[2] and trunks: the king was there present, but I did not see him. We passed through this court into several others, and afterwards came into the pagoda. The portal appeared be most ancient and very well wrought, the whole building indifferent handsome, and of the form of our churches in Europe. We saw several statues of brass gilt, which seemed to offer homage to a great idol all of gold, about forty foot high, in the side of which idol there were several other small ones, some of which, being also of gold, had lighted lamps fastened into them, from the

---

[1]   Choisy says it had "a head like an ugly woman, or rather like a whore; the lips were red, the face or snout rather white, but the eyes much lower than the nose" (1993: 170).

[2]   Tusks.

top to the bottom of them. At the end of this pagoda there is another great idol on a very stately tombstone.

I afterwards went into another pagoda adjoining to the first and I passed under a vault like a cloister where there were idols on each hand, every two feet, gilded, who had each of them a little lamp burning before them which the Talapoins, which are the priests of Siam, do light every night. In this pagoda was the mausoleum of the deceased queen who died about four or five years since. 'Tis magnificent enough, and behind this mausoleum was another of a king of Siam, represented by a great statue lying on one side and dressed as kings are wont to be in days of ceremony.[1] This statue is about twenty-five foot long, 'twas of brass gilt. I went farther into other places where there were a great many of these statues, both of gold and silver: several had rich diamond rings and rubies on their fingers. I never saw so many images and so much gold. (The whole was but fine because of the display of so much wealth.)

I afterwards went to see the elephants; there is a great number of them, and who are of a prodigious size. I saw a piece of cannon, cast at Siam, of eighteen foot long, (fourteen inches in diameter at its mouth,) and that would carry balls of three hundred pound weight; there is a great many cannons which the Siamese make themselves in this kingdom.

The 31st was (at Juthia or Siam) a day of rejoicing for the King of Portugal's coming to the crown,[2] which was solemnized by the letting off the guns and several shows of fireworks from on board the foreign vessels.

The next morning being the 1st of November, Mr Constance invited me to a great feast, which was made as a

[1]   Chaumont is presumably describing a sleeping Buddha.
[2]   Pedro II (1648-1706) who reigned from 1683.

further continuation of the former solemnity, to which I went, and all the Europeans in the town. The guns ceased not from firing all that day. After dinner there was a comedy, the Chinese began it and there were Siamese in it, [but] their postures seemed to me ridiculous, and far unlike those of our buffoons in Europe; with the exception of two men who ascended to the top of two very high perches which had at their end a little apple,[1] and standing upright on the top of them, they showed several strange tricks. Afterwards we had a Chinese puppet play, but all of that was not equal to what one can see in Europe.

On the 4th, being Sunday, Mr Constance told me that the king was to go to the pagoda where he is wont to go every year, and prayed me to see him pass by, (having prepared a pavilion for me over the water). I went with him and all my attendants; and having remained there a while, there appeared a great gilded barge, in which was a mandarin who came to see whether all things were in order: scarcely was he passed by but I saw several barges wherein were mandarins of the first rank who were all of them in suits of red cloth; they are wont on these solemn days to be all clothed with the same colour, and 'tis the king who nominates; they had white bonnets on, very sharply pointed, and the *oyas* had at the bottom of their caps a golden band. As to their breeches, 'twas a kind of scarf, as I already said. After them came those of the second rank, the life guards, several soldiers, and then the king in a barge attended with two others which were very fine ones; the watermen of the three barges were apparelled like the soldiers, but only they had a kind of breast-plate, and each of them an helmet on their heads, which was said to be of gold. Their pagaies or sculls were gilt with gold, as all the

---

[1]   Hardly likely; more probably a local fruit.

barges were, which showed very fine. There were an hundred and four-score and five rowers in each of these barges, and in those of the mandarins about an hundred, and an hundred and twenty; there were life guards that followed, and several other mandarins who made the rear guard. The king was richly apparelled with several precious stones. I saluted him in passing by, and he returned my compliment. His train consisted of an hundred and forty stately barges, which appeared very fine indeed on the water, passing all in good order. After dinner I went into my barge to see the rest of the ceremony. At night the king changed his barge, and proposed a prize to that barge that should first arrive by force of oars to the palace. He himself was one of the party, and he advanced by much before the others; for that his rowers won the money. I know not how great 'twas. The other barges passed on very swiftly in no order; all the river was covered with them who came to see the king, that day being designed for his showing himself to his people. I believe there were an hundred thousand to see him.[1]

At night there were fireworks for joy of the coronation of the King of England;[2] the whole affair was well carried on, and the foreign vessels fired from all parts their cannon.

On the 5th this feast continued and the cannon was fired throughout the day. Mr Constance invited me to dinner where all the Europeans were.

On the 8th the king departed for Louvo,[3] which is a country seat where he generally remains for eight or nine months in the year, it being distant twenty leagues from Siam.[4]

[1] Choisy says 200,000.
[2] James II (r.1685-88).
[3] Lopburi.
[4] The capital city of Siam, Ayutthaya, commonly also called Siam by Europeans.

On the 15th I departed for that place. I lay in the way at a house which was built for me; 'twas in the same form as that where I had been lodged since I left my vessel up to the city of Siam. 'Twas near a residence where the king lies when he goes to Louvo. I remained there all the 16th[1] and on the 17th set out thither, where I arrived the same day at eight at night.

---

[1]   Choisy gives the reason for this: the ambassador's house in Lopburi was not yet ready for him.

CHAPTER FOUR

At Louvo

I found [my] house quite well built after the fashion of the country;[1] in your entrance to it you must pass through a garden, where there are several fountains. In this garden you ascend five or six steps, and you go to a reception room standing very high where you take the air. I found here a fine chapel, and a lodging for all those who attended me.

On Monday the 19th the king gave me a particular audience. After dinner I went abroad to take the air on elephants, whose goings are very uneasy and incommodious. I had rather ride ten leagues on horseback than one on these animals.

On the 23rd Mr Constance told me the king would give me the divertisement of a combat of elephants, and entreated me to bring along with me the captains of the ships who had conducted me, to show them the sport, who were the Sieurs de Vaudricourt and Joyeux; we went thither on elephants and the fight was carried on after the same manner as that which I above related.

---

[1] The 1687 translation was imaginative when describing the ambassador's residence in Lopburi, saying it was built in the Moorish fashion and had a summer-house.

The king sent for these two captains and told them he was very glad they were the King of France's first captains who came into his kingdom, and he wished them as happy a return as their arrival was. He gave each of them a sabre whose handle and guard was of gold, and the sheath almost entirely covered with the same metal, a golden filigree chain cleverly wrought (and very thick, as though to serve as a baldric), and a vest of cloth of gold with gold buttons; as Mr de Vaudricourt was the chief captain, so his present was richer and better. The king gave him notice to have a care of their enemies by the way; they answered that His Majesty furnished them with arms to defend themselves, and that they would acquit themselves of their duty. The captains spake to him without lighting off their elephants; I saw very well that under pretence of a combat of elephants, he was minded to make these presents to the captains in the sight of several Europeans who were present, to give a public mark of the particular distinction he would make of the French nation, (and I also learned that the king gave that same day audience to the heads of the English [East India] Company, and that they were obliged to conform to the manner of the country, that is to say prostrating themselves on the ground and shoeless).

The king afterwards returned, and I went to see an elephant which had been brought by the females who are instructed to go into the woods with a man or two to conduct them, as far as twenty-five or thirty leagues, to seek wild elephants, and when they have found any, they so order it as to draw them on to a place near the town designed to receive them. 'Tis a great space dug in the earth, and surrounded by a wall of brick very high. There is also a second enclosure of great stakes, about fifteen foot high, through which a man may easily pass, and a double gate with similar stakes of the same height, which shuts of itself by means of a sliding door, so that when an elephant is within, he cannot get out. The female elephants do first enter, the wild ones follow them, and after they are inside the sliding door is closed.

This same day Mr Constance presented the two captains of the king's vessels with several (porcelains,) Japan works,[1] silver and other curiosities.

On Saturday the 24th I got on horseback to go see the wild elephants taken.

The king being come to the end of this place which is enclosed with stakes and a wall, there entered a man who went with a staff to attack the wild elephant, who at the same time left the females, and pursued him. The man continued this management, and thus busied this elephant, till the females who were with him got out of the place by the gate, which was immediately shut after them, and the elephant seeing himself left alone imprisoned, grew enraged. The fellow set upon him again, and instead of flying on that side which he was wont, he ran out of the gate, and the elephant followed him. When he was between the two gates he was shut in; and being hot they threw a great deal of water on his body, and there were several elephants brought to him, who carressed him with their trunks to comfort him, as it were. They tied his two hind legs, and the gate was opened to him, he marched five or six paces, and found four elephants of war, and one to confront him to make him show respect, two others who were at his sides, and one behind to push him with his head; they brought him in this manner under a roof, beneath which there was placed a great post, to which he was tied. He was left with two elephants placed on each side to tame him, and the others were led away. When the wild elephants have remained fifteen days in this manner, they know them who are wont to feed them, and follow

---

[1] Lacquered ware.

them, so that in a short while they become as tractable as the others. The king has a great many of these females who do nothing else but decoy these wild ones.

On Monday the 25th I went to see a tiger fight with three elephants, but the tiger was not the strongest, he received a blow with a tooth that carried away half his jaw.[1]

Tuesday the 26th I had particular audience, this being the fourth time, and the king continued to show me the esteem he had for the French nation, after several other discourses, of which I have given our king an account. At night I went to see a feast, which the Siamese celebrate at the beginning of their year, which is attended with great lights. It's performed in the palace, in a great court, round about which there are several cabinets full of little lamps, and before these cabinets there are perches drove into the ground, where hang several painted horn lanterns; this feast lasts eight days.

On Sunday the 2nd of December, Mr Constance sent me some presents; he did the same also to the Abbé de Choisy, and the gentlemen which accompanied me. The presents were (porcelains), bracelets, China cabinets, nightgowns, and Japan works made of silver, bezoar stones, rhinoceros horns, and other curiosities of that country.

On the 10th I went to see the great hunting of elephants, which is in this following form: the king sends a great

---

[1] Choisy wrote on 26 November "We have seen a fight between three elephants and a tiger. The contest was unequal. The elephants had a leather mask over their faces, behind which they curled up their trunks, and they attacked the tiger with their tusks. The tiger sometimes threw itself on their masks; he bit the leg of one elephant who cried out a lot. Finally the tiger, either worn out or cowardly, gave up and appeared to be dead. The elephants went to turn him over gently, and sometimes he picked himself up. These poor elephants obeyed the voices of their mahouts and pushed hard when they were told."

numbers of female elephants into the countryside together, and when they have been several days in the wood, and he is informed they have found elephants, he sends thirty or forty thousand men, who make a very great ring in the place where the elephants are, (the men are posted four by four, from twenty to twenty-five feet distant from each other,) and each company has a fire raised about three foot high or thereabouts. There is also another ring of elephants of war, distant from one another about an hundred or an hundred and fifty paces, and in those places where the elephants may more easily pass through, the elephants of war are more numerous. In several places there is cannon which is fired at the wild elephants when they will force a passage, for they are in great fear of fire. Every day this enclosure or ring is lessened, and at length 'tis very small, and the fires are then only five or six paces from each other. These elephants hearing noise about them dare not fly, although now and then one or two do escape, for I was told that some days past there were ten got away. When they are to be taken they are made to enter into a place surrounded with stakes, where there are some trees, through which a man may easily pass. There is also another ring of elephants of war and soldiers, among which there are men mounted on elephants, who dexterously throw cords at the elephants' hind feet, who when they are fastened in this manner are brought between two tame elephants, besides which there is another who pushes on them from behind, so they are obliged to march, and when one is unruly, the others strike him with their trunks. They bring them next beneath a roof, where they are fastened in the same fashion as before. I saw ten taken in this hunt, and I was told there were an hundred and forty in the ring; the king was there present and gave orders for what was necessary.

In this place I had the honour to have a long conference with him, and he prayed me to leave Mr de Forbin, the lieutenant of my ship, with him, which I agreed to,[1] and presented him. After the king had spoken with him, he presented him with a sabre, whose handle and guard was of gold, and the sheath studded with the same, with a justaucorps[2] of gold-threaded European brocade with gold buttons. Then the king presented me with a covered golden cup and saucer, and ordered that I be served a collation in a grove, where I had excellent preserves, wine and fruit.

The next morning being the 11th I returned to this hunt, being mounted on an elephant. The king was again there on this day, and sent two mandarins to me, to desire me to come to him. He spake several things to me, and entreated me to leave Mr de La Mare, the engineer,[3] behind to fortify some places. I told him I did not doubt but the king my master would be content I should leave him, seeing His Majesty's interests were very dear to him, and he was an able man who should satisfy His Majesty. I thereupon ordered Monsieur de La Mare to remain in Siam to give service to the king, who desired to speak with him, and gave him a vest of stuff of gold. The king told me he would send a little elephant to the Duke of Burgundy, which he showed me, and having a while thought of it, he said that if he should give one only to the Duke of Burgundy, he feared

---

[1] The Chevalier de Forbin (spelt 'Fourbin' by both Chaumont and Choisy) had to be ordered to remain in Siam, he being most unwilling to stay. He maintained Phaulkon wished to prevent him telling Louis XIV of the real state of wealth in the country.

[2] Jerkin.

[3] La Mare was to stay and draw up detailed plans for the fortifications of several Siamese cities. According to Choisy, the request for La Mare occurred on 10 December at the same time as Forbin was formally offered.

lest the Duke of Anjou[1] should take it ill, and therefore he would send two. Designing to depart the next morning to go on board, I presented the gentlemen to him who were with me to take leave of His Majesty; they saluted him, and the king wished them a good voyage. The Bishop of Metellopolis would have presented him the Abbé de Lionne and Le Vachet, Missionaries, who were going to France with me, to take their leave of him, but he told the bishop that, as to those two persons, they were of his family, and that he considered them as his children, and that they should take their leave of him in his palace. Afterwards the king retired, and I attended on him to the end of the wood taking the way of Louvo, because the king had a house in the wood, where he usually tarries whilst he is busied in this elephant hunt.

On Wednesday the 12th the king gave me audience of leave. The bishop was there. He was pleased to say he was very well satisfied with me and with all my negotiation; he gave me a great golden vessel, which they call a bosset,[2] and this is one of the most honourable marks of the king's favour. (It was as if the King of France bestowed the title of ducal ruler). He told me he would not have the accustomed ceremonies about it, because there might be something which would not please me, by reason of the genuflections which the greatest of the kingdom are obliged to make on this occasion. There is no stranger in his court, excepting the King of Cambodia's nephew, who has received the like mark of honour, which signifies that one is an *oyas*, a

---

[1] The Dukes of Burgundy and Anjou were grandsons of Louis XIV; these "pocket-sized elephants", in Choisy's words, had to be off-loaded at the last minute, as there was simply no room for them among the three hundred bales of presents being transported on the two French ships.

[2] Golden betel-nut box.

dignity which according to what I have just said is like that of a duke of France;[1] there are several sorts of *oyas*, which are distinguished by their bossets. This monarch had the goodness to tell me several things in such an obliging manner that I dare not relate them; and in all my voyage I received such great honours from him that I should scarce be believed, were they not solely due to the character His Majesty has been pleased to honour me with. I received also a thousand civilities from his ministers, and the rest of the court. The Abbé de Lionne and Le Vachet took at the same time their leaves of the king, who having wished them a good voyage, gave each of them a golden crucifix mixed with tambac, which is a metal more esteemed than gold in that country, the foot of it being silver.

At the end of the audience, Monsieur Constance carried me into a parlour surrounded by water-spouts which was in the palace enclosure, where I found a table very well spread, after the manner of the kingdom of Siam. The king had the goodness to send me two or three dishes from his table, for he dined at the same time. (One was rice arranged in their fashion, and the two others dried and salted fish from Japan.) About five of the clock I went into a gilt chair, carried by ten men, and the gentlemen who accompanied me rode on horseback. We entered into our barks, and were attended by a great many mandarins, the streets were lined with soldiers, elephants, and Moorish cavaliers. 'Twas the same also in the morning, when I had my last audience. All the mandarins that accompanied me to my barge went into theirs, and came with me; there were about an hundred barges, and I arrived the next morning, being the 13th, at [the city of] Siam about three in the morning.

---

[1]   This repeats an earlier remark. La Loubère lists the seven ranks of nobility as "Pa-ya, Oc-ya, Oc-Pra, Oc-Louang, Oc-Counne, Oc-Meuing, and Oc-Pan" (1693: 79).

CHAPTER FIVE

Departure from Siam

The King of Siam's letter and his ambassadors for France were with me, in a very stately barge attended by several others. The king made me several presents amongst which (were pieces of porcelain worth six or seven hundred *pistoles*, two pairs of Chinese screens, four Chinese cloth of gold and silver table coverings), a crucifix, the body of which is gold, a cross of tambac, (and with the foot made of silver,) together with several other curiosities of the Indies. The custom of these countries being to gratify those who bring the presents, I gave to the steersmen of the king's barges about eight or nine hundred *pistoles*. As to Mr Constance, I took the liberty to give him (an item of furniture which I had brought from France, worth more than a thousand *écus*, a very fine sedan chair which had cost me two hundred *écus* in France), and to Madame his wife (a mirror embellished with gold and precious stones worth about sixty *pistoles*). (I have omitted to say that) the King of Siam also gave presents to the value of seven or eight hundred *pistoles* to the Abbé de Choisy in China cabinets, silver Japan works, (several very fine pieces of porcelain), and other Indian curiosities.[1]

[1] As can be seen, the value of presents in the seventeenth century was carefully calculated and in no ways kept secret.

On the 14th at five of the clock at night, I departed from [the city of] Siam accompanied by Mr Constance, several mandarins, and a great many barges, and arrived at Bangkok the next morning; the forts which we found on the way, and those of Bangkok, saluted me with all their artillery. I remained a day at Bangkok, because the king had told me that, being a soldier, he desired me I would view all the fortifications, and to tell his servants what it wanted to defend [the place] well, and to pitch on a place to build a church. I drew a small sketch and gave it to Mr Constance.

On the 16th in the morning I departed thence accompanied by mandarins, the forts saluted me again, and at four of the clock I arrived at the bar of Siam, in the chaloupes belonging to our king's two ships, on which I got on board.

On the 17th the King of Siam's frigate in which were the ambassadors (and the letter for the King of France) came and cast anchor near my ship. I sent my chaloupe, which brought two of the ambassadors, and I afterwards sent back the same chaloupe which brought the other ambassador, and the king's letter, which was on a very high dais or pyramid, gilded all over, written on a leaf of gold, rolled up, and put into a gold box. We saluted the letter with the firing of several pieces of cannon. 'Twas laid (on the poop of my ship with parasols above it until the day of our departure). When the mandarins passed it, they reverenced it after their manner, it being their custom to do the greatest honours they are able to the king's letter. The next morning the ship which had brought them left us, and went back again up the river, and at the same time appeared another ship of the King of Siam, which came and cast anchor near us, in which was Mr Constance. He came on board of me the next morning, being the 19th, where he dined, and afterwards he went to land in my chaloupe. I saluted him with twenty-one pieces of cannon and we parted with no small trouble, for we had begun a strict friendship, and treated one another with the greatest confidence. He is a person of great sense and merit.

I was astonished to hear no news of Mr Le Vachet (Missionary, the head of the French [East India] Company), and of my secretary,[1] who were to have been on board, having been informed that they [de]parted from the River of Siam on the 16th with seven gentlemen who were to accompany the King of Siam's ambassadors, and several of their domestics. This made me think they were lost, and made me resolve not to tarry for them, for the wind was favourable; but Mr Constance desired me to have patience one day, whilst he would send along the coast for news of them.

The next morning, being the 20th, part of these people came on board, four of the gentlemen belonging to the King of Siam's ambassadors, and most of their domestics having been unwilling to embark themselves in a boat they had gotten by the way, because 'twas too low in the water. They told me that the same day, being the 16th, they came near our vessel at eleven at night, and thinking to cast anchor, they had not rope enough in their boat, which they perceived in seeing the boat fall off from the vessel. Then there arose a great wind which made the waves arise, and the currents ran against them, which carried them more than forty leagues out at sea, with great danger of being cast away. They told us they had left the others about twenty-five leagues off from where we were, upon a muddy bank, so that they are not to be expected so soon, which made me resolve not to go away before next morning.

---

[1]   The Sieur de La Brosse-Bonneau, brother of André Deslandes-Boureau, who had begun French commercial relations with Siam in 1680. La Brosse-Bonneau is mentioned by name later in the text.

I believe I ought in this place to speak of the Jesuits which were embarked with us at Brest, and whom we left at Siam. They were Fathers Fontaney, Tachard, Gerbillon, Le Comte, Bouvet, and another,[1] religious men of virtue and learning, whom our king had chosen to send to China to make mathematical observations. I think I am bound in justice to say of them that when we were arrived to the Cape of Good Hope, the Dutch governor was very kind to them, and gave them an house in the garden belonging to the Company,[2] very fitting to make their observations in, where they carried all their mathematical instruments; but as I remained but six or seven days in this place, they had not time to make a great many. These Fathers have been very useful to me in my voyage to Siam, by their piety, their good example, and the pleasantness of their conversation. I had every day near five or six masses said on board ship, and had set apart a chamber for that purpose. All the festivals and Sundays we had a sermon, or a short exhortation. Father Tachard, one of them, catechized the

---

[1]   Father Jean de Fontaney (1643-1710), head of the party, a former teacher at the College of Louis le Grand, went twice to China, cured Emperor Kiangxi of an illness, and finally left in 1703 to teach in La Flèche. Guy Tachard (1651-1712) was considered by many the evil genius of the French imbroglio in Siam, to which he paid several visits; he was to return with Chaumont's embassy with secret instructions from Phaulkon to negotiate with Louis XIV's confessor, Father de La Chaize. Jean-François Gerbillon (1654-1707) was to succeed Verbiest in the friendship of Emperor Kiangxi. Louis Le Comte (1655-1728), a gifted preacher, stayed in Siam at Phaulkon's insistence and served for a time as his secretary before going to China. Joachim Bouvet (1656-1730) was in Peking until 1793 and returned to Paris in 1697, then went back to China with eight more Jesuits, and studied Chinese texts. "Another" Jesuit was Claude de Visdelou (1656-1737), a teacher like Fontaney, who was to work in China and Pondichéry.
[2]   The VOC, the Dutch East India Company.

whole ship's company three times a week, and the same Father has done much good in the ship; for discoursing familiarly with the seamen and soldiers, there's not one of them but performs his devotions frequently. He composed all differences which arose amongst them. (There were [also] two Huguenot sailors, who by his care abjured the heresy before Father de Fontaney, who was the superior [of the Jesuits].)[1] The Fathers went to Siam intending to embark themselves on Portugal vessels, which are to be met with commonly at Macao, and which return to China. They found [in Siam] Mr Constance, the King of Siam's minister, who very much loves the Jesuits, and protects them (and received them very favourably). He had entertained them at Louvo, in one of the king's houses, and defrayed all their charges.

In an audience which the king gave me, I told him I had brought with me six Jesuits, who intended for China to make mathematical observations, and that they had been chosen by the king my master as the most capable in this science. He told me he would see them, and was very glad they were reconciled with the Bishop of Metellopolis; he has spoke to me several time on that subject.[2] Mr Constance presented them to him four or five days later, and by good hap[3] for them there was an eclipse of the moon. The king bid them bring along with them their mathematical instruments into a house where he was going to lie, a

---

[1]   The excessive piety on board ship, and the constant meddling of Father Tachard (he had routed out the two Huguenots and 'converted' them by 13 May) must have made the journey somewhat tedious for the crew, as Choisy on occasions implies.

[2]   The Jesuits and the Missionaries (led by the Bishop of Metellopolis) were at first in open dispute. Chaumont glosses over the rifts between the mostly Portuguese Jesuits in Ayutthaya and the French Missionaries, which had already reached the ears of King Narai.

[3]   Luck.

league off of Louvo, where he commonly is when he takes the pleasure of hunting.[1] The Fathers failed not to come there, and planted themselves with their telescopes in a gallery, where the king came about three of the clock in the morning, which was the time of the eclipse.[2] They made him see in their telescope all the effects of the eclipse, which did much please him; he showed them much respect, and told them he knew Mr Constance was their friend, as well as Father de La Chaize.[3] He gave them a great crucifix of gold and of tambac, and bid them to send it from him to Father de La Chaize; he gave another smaller to Father Tachard, telling them he would see them another time. Seven or eight days before my departure, Mr Constance proposed the Fathers that if two of them would remain at Siam the king would be very glad of it. They answered they could not, being ordered by the King of France to make what haste they could to China. He answered, this being so, they must write to the general of their order to send a dozen of them as soon as he could to Siam, the king having told him he would build them observatories, houses, and churches. Father de Fontaney made this proposition known to me. I told him he could not do better than accept of this offer, seeing in the end this must turn to a great advantage (for the conversion of the kingdom). He told me upon my encouragement he intended to send Father Tachard into France on this occasion, which I approved of, Father Tachard being a man of great wit, and who would undoubtedly effect this business, letters not being sufficient to remove several objections which might be raised, wherefore I brought him home with me. The Father has

[1] At Thale Chupson, just outside Lopburi, where Phaulkon was to be tortured and executed in June 1688.
[2] Tachard makes much of this occasion graced by the royal presence.
[3] Louis XIV's Jesuit confessor.

moreover much assisted me, as also the gentlemen which accompanied me, whom he taught mathematics very diligently during our voyage.

I shall say nothing of the great qualities of the Bishop of Metellopolis, nor of the progress of the Foreign Missions in the East, seeing that according to their custom they will not fail to give the public a full relation of what concerns the [Catholic] religion in those countries. I should have great satisfaction to have met there with the Bishop of Heliopolis;[1] the King of Siam told me one day he would have died from joy to have seen an ambassador in his kingdom from France; but it did not please God to give either of us that consolation, and we were informed that he had ended in China his laborious enterprise in a very saintly death.

But before we relate what occurred after our departure from the kingdom of Siam until our arrival at Brest, I believe it will be convenient to give an account here of what I remarked (or learned from persons worthy of credit), during the small time I was in the kingdom, of the customs, government, commerce, and religion of this country.

---

[1]   François Pallu (1626-1684), Missionary; he worked first in France and then in Siam before going to China where he died.

A Siamese noble being carried by litter in Ayutthaya

OF THE GOVERNMENT, MANNERS, RELIGION AND COMMERCE OF THE KINGDOM OF SIAM, IN THE NEIGHBOURING COUNTRIES, AND SEVERAL OTHER PARTICULARITIES

PART II

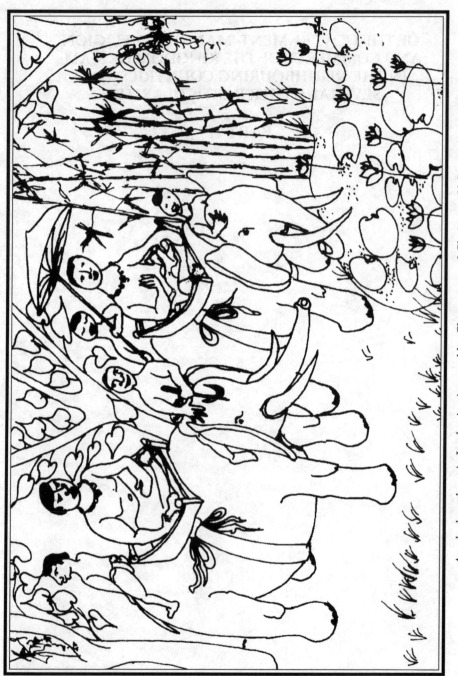

An elephant hunt in Lopburi, witnessed by Chaumont and Choisy on 11 December 1685

CHAPTER SIX

Justice, government, Mr Constance, and trade

Every day the mandarins whose duty is to render justice meet together in one of the halls in the palace of the King of Siam, where they hear causes. (This is like the Palais in Paris) where those that have any request to make stand at the door of this room, till they be called, and then they enter with their petition in their hands (and present it).

Foreigners who institute proceedings concerning trade goods offer their petition to the Barcalon, who is the king's chief minister, who judges all affairs concerning commerce and foreigners; in his absence, his usual deputy does it, and in both their absences a kind of alderman. There is an officer appointed to see after the taxes and tallage to whom one addresses oneself. When affairs have been examined, an account thereof is given to the officers within the palace, who relate the same to the king.

After the council has assembled and he has seated himself on a throne three spans high, all the mandarins prostrate themselves with their faces on the ground; and the Barcalon, or others of the chief *oyas*, acquaint the king with the affairs under discussion, and their judgments thereupon, which His Majesty pronounces, confirms or alters according to his will. In matters of great consequence, he causes the case to be brought into the palace, and afterwards sends to the disputants his judgment in writing. The mandarins established by the king to administer justice are called according to their different offices Oyas Obras, Oyas Momrat, Oyas Campeng, Oyas Ricchou, Oyas Shaynan, Opran, Olvan, Oean, Omun.[1]

The king is a most absolute prince throughout his kingdom and a man may say him to be almost the Siamese god; they dare not out of respect call him by his name.[2] He punishes most severely the smallest crime, for his subjects wish be governed with the rod in hand. He sometimes even makes use of soldiers of his guard to punish the guilty, when their crime is extraordinary, and sufficiently proved. Those who are commonly employed in these sort of executions are an hundred and fifty soldiers, or thereabouts, who have their arms painted from the shoulder to the wrist.[3] The common punishment is thirty, forty, fifty or more stripes of the rattan upon the shoulder of the criminal, according to the greatness of the crime; others are pecked into the head with a sharp pointed iron. As to accomplices in a fault worthy of death, after the head has been cut off the real criminal, 'tis tied about the neck of the confederate, and is left exposed to the sun for three days and three nights without covering it, which gives a most filthy stink to him that carries it.

In this kingdom the Law of Talionis[4] is much used. The worst punishment was not long ago to condemn malefactors worthy of death to the river, which is such another

---

[1]   The information is suspect. See p. 66 for La Loubère's listing of ranks. Choisy, after naming the seven most important officials in the kingdom, gives the ranks of Ok-ia or Oya, Ok-Pra or Opra, Ok-luang, Ok-khun, and Ok-mun. Oyas Campeng may be the ruler of Kampengpetch, and Olvan may be the palace (wang) chamberlain.

[2]   This is true, though his name was known, as Gervaise makes clear.

[3]   The "painted arms" or pintos braços; they were in fact tattooed.

[4]   The Hammurabi law of "an eye for an eye, a tooth for a tooth".

kind of punishment like our galley slaves, or rather worse; but now they are punished with death.

The king minds building more than any of his predecessors, repairing the walls of towns, raising up pagodas, and adorning his palace, building houses for foreigners, and ships after the European fashion.[1] He is very kind to all those who withdraw into his country, taking them into his service.

The kings of Siam were not wont to let themselves be seen as often as this does; they lived almost alone, and this present king did like the others (at the beginning of his reign). But Mgr de Bérythe,[2] the apostolic vicar, made use of a certain Brahmin,[3] who being a kind of joker, had great liberty of speaking to this monarch, by whose means he gave the prince to understand the power and manner of the government of our great monarch, and at the same time the custom of all the kings of Europe to be seen by their subjects and foreigners; and having considered this matter, he thought fit to send for Mgr de Bérythe, and afterwards several others; since which time he is become affable and accessible to strangers.

Heretofore when the kings would not let themselves be seen, the ministers did what they pleased, but the present king who as I have said wants not in judgment, and is a great politician, will be ignorant of nothing; he has fixed to him Mr Constance, of whom I have several times spoken. He is a Greek by nation, a person of great penetration and

---

[1] Indeed Narai's building orgy can be compared to that of Louis XIV, though it was not on the scale of that of Jayavarman VII of Cambodia at the end of the twelfth century.

[2] Bishop of Berithus, Lambert de la Motte (1624-1679), who founded the Missionary Seminary of the Far East in Siam.

[3] Most likely a court Brahmin, but unlikely to have filled the role of court jester; more an astrologer.

vivacity of spirit, and extraordinary prudence. He can and does do all things under the king's authority in the kingdom, but this minister would never accept of the greatest offices which the king has offered him several times. The Barcalon who died about two years since,[1] who by right of his place had the management of all affairs of state, was a person of very great abilities, that acquitted himself well in his employments, and was greatly beloved by the people. He that succeeded him was a Malay by nation,[2] which is a country near to Siam. He made great use of Mr Barron,[3] an Englishman, to bring the king into an ill opinion of Mr Constance, but the king understood the other's malice, caused him to be cudgelled until he was left for dead, and dispossessed him of his office; he that enjoys it at present lives in good intelligence with Mr Constance.

As by the laws introduced by the priests of the idols, who are called Talapoins, 'tis not allowable to kill, so malefactors of some enormous crime were heretofore con-

[1] The *Phra Klang*, Chao Phya Kosathipodi (brother of the future ambassador Kosa Pan, who became *Phra Klang* to King Petracha on King Narai's death), died in July 1683 in disgrace, contrary to Chaumont's assertions. Like many foreigners, Chaumont had an exaggerated opinion of the importance of the Barcalon.

[2] Ok-ya Wang, the successor of Kosathipodi, had formerly acted as grand Siamese admiral for three years in Pattani, and fell from royal favour after some two years in office. His assistant who brought charges against Phaulkon had his head cut off. He was succeeded by a front man, Okya Phra Sedet, who was also the 'Grand Mandarin of the Talapoins'.

[3] According to Hutchinson (*Adventurers in Siam in the Seventeenth Century*, 1940), Samuel Barron was sent by Phaulkon to command a trading vessel to Tonkin, and was offered further employment, but refused continued involvement with "the Greek's villany". Barron made approaches to Bishop Laneau for his protection, and advised England to declare war on Siam. Sir John (not Sir Joseph) Child, in charge in Surat, sent his own envoys to Ayutthaya in 1685 to assess the situation, by when the French had the upper hand.

demned to the chain for life, or led into some deserts to perish there with hunger, whereas this present king causes their heads to be struck off and throws them to elephants.

The king has spies throughout all his kingdom to know whether matters of any importance are concealed from him. He most severely chastises those who abuse their authority. Every foreign nation established in the Kingdom of Siam has particular officers, and the king takes of all these nations persons which he makes general officers throughout all his kingdom. There are many Chinese in his country; there were heretofore many Moors, but some years past he discovered so many foul treacheries among them, such frauds and enormities, that he required a great number of them to remove and go to other countries.[1]

The commerce of foreign merchants was heretofore very considerable; but since some years, the various revolutions which have happened in China, Japan, and other parts of the Indies have discouraged foreign merchants from coming in such great numbers. Yet 'tis hoped, seeing all these disturbances are quieted, trade will flourish again, and that the King of Siam by means of his minister will send his ships to take in the most precious and most rare commodities in all the Oriental kingdoms, and return all things to their first and flourishing state.

[1]   A reference to the misdeeds of the Persians (especially Aga Muhammad, who died in 1679), who were much in evidence before the rise to power of Phaulkon.

CHAPTER SEVEN

War, foreigners, and crafts

The Siamese make war after a very different manner from most nations, that is by driving their enemies out of their places, without doing them any further harm than making them slaves; and if they bear arms, it seems rather they intend to affright them by shooting into the ground or up into the air than to kill them, and if they do, 'tis rather to defend themselves out of necessity; but necessity to kill happens seldom, because almost all their enemies follow the same method and only lead to the same ends. There are companies and regiments who are detached from the rest during the night, who go into the enemies' villages, and lead away all the inhabitants captives, as well men, women as children to be made slaves. The king gives them lands and buffaloes to cultivate them, and when the king has need he makes use of them. These late years the king has made war against the revolted Cambodians, [who were] assisted by the Chinese and Cochin-Chinese, where he was forced to fight in earnest, and there were several soldiers killed on both sides, being instructed by European commanders to fight after our manner.

(They have a continual war with the Kingdom of Laos, the subject thereof being on account of a very rich Moor who went into that country on behalf of the King of Siam, and stayed there with considerable sums [of money belonging to him]. He was asked for of the King of Laos, who refused [to extradite] him, which made the King of Siam declare war on him.)

Before that war there was a great commerce between their states, and that of Siam drew great advantages by the great quantities of gold, musk, benzoin, elephants' teeth and other merchandise which came from Laos in exchange for linen and other goods.

The King of Siam is still at war with the King of Pegu; he has several slaves of this nation.

There are people of several foreign countries in his kingdom. The Moors were in great abundance, as I already said, but now several of them are fled into the Kingdom of Golconda[1] who were in the king's service, and have carried along with them above twenty thousand *catis*, each *cati* being worth fifty crowns.[2] The King of Siam wrote to the King of Golconda to send him back those fugitives, or oblige them to pay this sum, but the king [of Golconda] did not wish to do anything and would not listen (to the ambassadors he sent him), which has put the King of Siam on proclaiming a war against him, and taking a ship at the time when I was at Siam belonging to him, whose lading is valued at an hundred thousand crowns. There are six frigates commanded by English and French, who cruise on those coasts.[3]

Of late the Emperor of China has given leave to all strangers to come and negotiate in his kingdom; this permission is only for five years, but 'tis hoped it will be continued, seeing 'tis of great advantage to his country.

[1] A powerful city and state in India near modern Hyderabad, capital of the Shiah kingdom from 1512 to 1687.
[2] The French text specifies *écus*.
[3] The ships were Siamese under European captains.

The King of Siam has a great many Malays in his kingdom; they are Mohammedans, and good soldiers, yet their religion differs somewhat from the Moors. The Peguans are as numerous in the country as the originary Siamese. There are also a great many Laotians, especially towards the north. Here are also eight or nine families of native Portuguese, but of those which are called mestizos, above a thousand, that is to say those who are born of a Portuguese man and a Siamese woman.

The Dutch have there only one factory.[1] The English the same.[2] The French also.

The Cochin-Chinese are about an hundred families, most Christians. Among the Tonkinese there are seven or eight Christian families.

The Malays are in fairly great numbers, who are most of them slaves, and who consequently do not make a body [or independent community]. The Makassars, and several of the people of the Isle of Java, are there established, as also the Moors: under the name of these last are comprehended Turks, Persians, Moguls, Golcondans, and those of Bengal.

The Armenians make a separate body; they are fifteen or sixteen families, all Christians and Catholics. The greatest part of them are horsemen of the king's guard.[3]

As to the manners of the Siamese, they are a people very docile, which proceeds rather from their nature, which desires repose, than any other cause. The Talapoins forbid

---

[1]   This is surprisingly uninformative, as the Dutch trading house was substantial. Chaumont is only describing the establishment in the capital; the Dutch also had a godown below Bangkok at a place they called Amsterdam (near Prapadeng), and another at Nakhon Si Thammarat.

[2]   The English factory was closed at this juncture, after having been burnt down in December 1682.

[3]   Chaumont is the only person, in the five published accounts of the embassy, to mention an Armenian community in Ayutthaya.

the killing of all sorts of animals, yet when any others kill pullets or ducks, they eat their flesh, without troubling themselves who did the murder, or wherefore they were killed, and likewise with other animals.

The Siamese are generally chaste, having but one wife, but the rich people, such as the mandarins, have concubines who remain shut up all their lives. The people are (quite faithful and) trusty, and do not steal, but 'tis not the same with some of the mandarins. The Malays who are very numerous in this kingdom are a very base people, and great thieves.

In this kingdom are several Peguans, who have been taken in war; they are a more stirring and vigorous sort of people than the Siamese. The women are given to liberty, and their conversation is dangerous.

The Laotians people the fourth part of the Kingdom of Siam, and being one-half Chinese, they partake of their manners, their craft and inclinations to steal with cunning. Their women are white and beautiful, very familiar and consequently perilous. In the Kingdom of Laos, a man that meets a woman to salute her with the accustomed civility kisses her, and did he do otherwise he would offend her.

The Siamese, as well officers as mandarins, are generally rich, for they spend hardly anything, the king giving them servants, who are obliged to maintain themselves at their own cost, being as it were slaves. They are under an obligation to serve them for nothing half a year; and these masters having many of them, they make use of one part while the other rest themselves, but those who do not serve them pay them every year a sum of money. Their victuals are cheap, being only rice, fish, and a very little flesh, and there's plenty indeed of this in the country. Their clothes last them long, being entire pieces of stuff, which do not so soon wear out as our apparel, and cost very little. Most of the Siamese are masons, or carpenters, and there are very good workmen among them, exactly imitating the curious works of Europe (in carving and gilding). As to painting, they are ignorant of the use of it; there are carved works in their pagodas, and in their tombs, which are very stately.

They also do clever work with quicklime, which they soak in sap which they draw out of a tree found in the forests, which makes it so lasting that it endures an hundred or two hundred years, although exposed to the injury of the weather.

CHAPTER EIGHT

Religion, the priesthood, marriage and divorce

Their religion, to speak properly, is only a parcel of
fabulous tales, which serve only to bring respect and great
profit to the Talapoins, who recommend not so much any
virtue to them as that of giving them alms. They have laws,
which they strictly observe, at least outwardly. Their end in
all their good works is the hope of a happy transmigration
after their death into the body of a rich man, of a king or a
great lord, or of a docile animal, as a cow or sheep, for these
people believe in metempsychosis. They for this reason do
much esteem these animals, and dare not, as I have noted,
kill any of them, as knowing not but they may kill their
father or mother, or some other of their relations. The
Siamese believe in a hell, where great enormities are
severely punished, only for a time; as also a paradise,
wherein sublime virtues are rewarded in the heavens,
where having become angels for some time they afterwards
return into the body of some man or animal.

The Talapoins' business is to read, sleep, eat, sing, and
seek alms. They go every morning to present themselves in
front of the doors or barges of persons they know, and
stand there for a while with great reservedness, saying
nothing, holding their fans so that they cover half their
faces; if they see anyone disposed to give them anything,

they tarry till they have received it. They eat whatever is given them, whether pullets or any other flesh, but they never drink wine, at least before lay people. They perform no office nor prayers to any divinity. The Siamese believe there have been three great Talapoins who by their most sublime merits in several thousand transmigrations have become gods, and having been so, have moreover acquired such great merits that they have been wholly annihilated; which is the term of the greatest merit and the greatest recompense obtainable, being no longer tired by their frequent changes of bodies. The last of these three Talapoins is the greatest god of the Siamese whom they call Nacodon,[1] because he has been in five thousand bodies. In one of these transmigrations, from a Talapoin he became a cow, and his brother would have killed him several times. But there needs a great book to describe the miracles which they say nature and not God wrought for his preservation. In short, this brother was thrown into hell for his great sins, where Nacodon caused him to be crucified; and for this reason they abominate the image of Christ on the cross, saying we adore the image of this brother of their great god who was crucified for his crimes.

This Nacodon being annihilated like the two others, they have no god at present, yet the law of this last remains, but only among the Talapoins, who affirm that after several centuries there will be an angel who will become a Talapoin, and afterwards a sovereign God, who by his great merits may come to be annihilated. These are the principles of their creed; for 'tis not to be imagined they adore the idols which are in their pagodas as divinities, but honour them only as men of great deserts, whose souls are at

---

[1] A corruption of the Buddha's name, Siddhartha Gautama, which Choisy rendered as Sommono-Ckodom and Tachard as Sommonokhodom.

present in some king, cow, or Talapoin. And herein consists their religion, which to speak properly acknowledges no God (and which only attributes all recompense for virtue to virtue itself, which has in its power to make happy the person who has received in his body or in that of some cow the soul of some powerful and rich lord.) Vice, say they, carries with it its own punishment, making the soul pass into the body of some vile fellow, or hog, or crow, or tiger, or such like cruel or otherwise less valued animal among them. They admit of angels, which they believe to have been the souls of just and good Talapoins; as to demons, they say, they have been the souls of wicked persons.

The Talapoins are much reverenced by all the people, and even by the king himself; they cast not themselves on the ground when they speak to him, as the greatest in the kingdom do, and the king and persons of highest quality salute them first. When these Talapoins thank anyone, they put their hand near to their forehead, and as to the common people they salute them not at all. They are apparelled like other Siamese, excepting that their sash is yellow, their legs and feet naked, they wear no hats, they carry over their heads a fan, made of a large palm leaf, to keep them from the sun which is very hot. They make but one true meal a day, to wit in the morning, and they eat at night perhaps some bananas or some figs, or other fruits.[1] They may leave when they will the Talapoin's dress and marry, having no other engagement on them but only to wear a yellow sash, and when they leave it, they are at liberty; and this makes them so numerous, that they are almost one third of the kingdom. That which they sing in the pagodas are some fabulous stories, larded with now and then a fine sentence; those which they sing during funerals of the dead are, "We must all die, we are all mortal." Dead bodies are burnt to

[1]   In theory they took no food after midday until the next morning.

the sound of bagpipes and other instruments. These funerals are very costly, and after the bodies are burnt, their ashes are put under great pyramids,[1] all gilded, raised about their pagodas.

The Talapoins practice a kind of confession; for their novices go at sunrise to prostrate themselves, or sit on their heels, mumbling some few words; after which one of the old Talapoins lifts up his hand on the side of his cheek, and gives him a kind of benediction; which done, the novice retires. When they preach, they exhort the people to be charitable to them, and suppose themselves very able fellows when they can cite some passages out of their ancient books, written in the Pali language, which is like Latin among us; for this language is fine and emphatical, having its conjugations like Latin.

When the Siamese intend to marry, the man's kindred go first to sound the maid's kindred's inclination, and when they have agreed on the business, the man's parents present seven bossets or boxes of betel and areca to the maid's relations; should they accept of them, they are already esteemed as married. Yet it may be broke off (and neither side can bring an action before a judge if they separate after this ceremony.)

Some days after the man's relations present him, and he himself offers more bossets than before, (the customary number being ten or fourteen), and then he who would marry remains in the house of his father-in-law, without there being any consummation, but only to see the maid and to accustom himself little by little to living with her for one or two months. After this all the relatives meet (with the elders of the group or nation), when they put into a

---

[1] Stupa or *chedi*; all the French travellers of the seventeenth century talked of pyramids.

purse, one a ring, and another bracelets, and another money; there are others who lay pieces of stuff on the centre of the table. In fine, the most ancient of the company takes a lighted taper and carries it seven times round these presents, whilst all the assembly shouts, wishing the spouses a happy marriage, perfect health, and long life. They afterwards eat and drink together and so the marriage is finished. As to the portion, 'tis as in France, excepting that the young man's relations carry his money to the maid's relations; but all this turns to the same, for the maid's portion is laid apart, and the whole is given to the new married couple to increase its worth.

If the husband puts away his wife without any form of justice, he loses the money that had been given him; if he repudiates her by the judge's sentence, who never refuses it, the woman's relations give him her portion. If there be any children, the boy follows the mother, and the girl the father; if there be two boys, and two girls, one boy and one girl live with the father, and one of each with the mother.[1]

---

[1] La Loubère, in his much fuller chapter (Part II, ch.VII) 'Concerning the Marriage and Divorce of the Siameses' in his *New Historical Relation of the Kingdom of Siam* does not agree: he maintains that the mother has the first, third, and fifth children, the father the even-born ones, and when there is an unequal number, the mother has the extra child (1693: 53).

CHAPTER NINE

Money, defences, trade, and the extent of the kingdom

(With regard to money, they use no gold, the largest silver piece being called a tical, and worth about forty *sous*; next comes the mayon, which weighs a quarter of a tical, and is worth ten *sous*, after is the fuang, worth five *sous*, the fourth is the sompaye, worth two and a half *sous*, and finally for the lowest currency are the cowries, which are shells brought them by the Dutch from the Maldives, Cochin-China or other coasts, eight hundred of these shells being worth a fuang, which is, [as noted] five *sous*.)

As to the strong places in the kingdom, there's Bangkok, which is about ten leagues from the mouth of the river Menam, where there are two forts, as I already mentioned. The capital city of Siam, called Juthia, is being newly fortified by an enclosure of brick walls. Corsuma,[1] a frontier town lying near the Kingdom of Cambodia, is but a weak place, and so is Tenasserim, on the side of Malabar.[2]

[1] Nakhon Ratchasima, given in La Loubère's map as Corazema, and in his text as "Corazema, which some do call Carissima". Choisy wrote of Conrasema. Both list several provincial towns in addition to those mentioned by Chaumont.

[2] Giving onto the Andaman Sea, and trading with the Malabar coast (on the south-western side of India).

(Mergui[1] is not fortified at all, but could easily be so, and a good port could be built there. Porcelut[2] is on the Laos frontier, and is not much fortified. Chainat[3] has the name of a town, and there remains some appearance of barriers, which formerly served for walls. Louvo, where the King of Siam remains nine months a year to take pleasure in hunting elephants and tigers, was formerly a grouping of pagodas surrounded by terraces, but this prince has made it incomparably more beautiful by the buildings he has caused to be constructed there, and has further much embellished it by bringing water in from the mountains.)

(Pattani[4] is one of the finest ports on the Malay coast, from where great commerce can be conducted. The King of Siam has refused both the English and Dutch [East India] Companies to set up there. An important establishment could be set up there which would be more advantageous than at [Judia, also called] Siam, because of its situation. The Chinese go there and so do several other nations. The river bank there could be easily fortified. This place belongs to a queen who is tributary to the King of Siam, who to speak properly is almost its master.)

As to their soldiers, 'twas not the custom to pay them, but this present king, having understood that the kings of Europe paid their men, wished the calculation of how much the pay of one fuang a day, which is five *sous*, would come to; but being informed by his treasurers what an immense sum 'twould cost him, by reason of the multitude of his soldiers, he changed this pay into rice, which he distributed to them since, (he having sufficient for their board); and they were therewith all well contented, for heretofore every

---

1   'Mere' in the French text.
2   Phitsanulok, in the centre-north.
3   In the central valley, above Ayutthaya.
4   'Patang' in the French text; it ceased to be a trading port of note at the beginning of the seventeenth century.

soldier was bound to furnish himself with rice (and to carry it with his arms, which inconvenienced him greatly).

As to their boats and vessels, their barges of state are the finest in the world, being made of one piece of timber, and are of a prodigious length, some of them holding from fifty to an hundred and an hundred and fourscore rowers; the two ends are high raised, (and he who steers by stamping at the poop causes the whole barge to shake, like a horse in jumping. They are all gilded with very fine carving,) and in the midst of them there is a seat like a throne, built like a pyramid, (very finely carved and gilded overall; there are more than a hundred different ornamentations, but all are perfectly gilded and very fine).

Heretofore they had only vessels built like those of China, (which are called junks,) some of which they use still to go into Japan, China and Tonkin; but the king has caused several to be built after the European fashion, and has bought some of the English (all approved and fitted out). There are about fifty galleys to guard the rivers and coasts; his galleys are not like those of France, there being but one man to an oar, and they are about forty, or fifty, at most, one each; (the rowers serve as soldiers). The king virtually only uses Moors, Chinese and Malabars to navigate, (and if he includes some Siamese as sailors, they are but few in number, and to learn the [art of] navigation.) The commanders of his ships are either English or French, by reason of the other nations' unskilfulness.

He sends every year to China five or six of these vessels known as junks, of which there are from a thousand to fifteen hundred tons, laden with cloth, coral, and divers other commodities from the coasts of Coromandel and Surat,[1] such as saltpetre, tin, and silver; he draws thence

---

[1]   The Coromandel coast is on the south-eastern side of India, and Surat on the western, above Bombay.

raw silks, silk lengths, satins, tea, musk, rhubarb, porcelains, varnished works, China wood, gold, and rubies. As
his subjects make use of several roots in physic, including
different kinds of sulphates, that brings him great profits.

The king sends to Japan two or three junks, but smaller
than the others, laden with (the same) merchandise (as for
China), and there is no need of sending money; (the goods
taken there are the least important, and the cheapest), such
as hides of all sorts (of animals which sell well there). This
is the best trade to be obtained in that place. In return they
obtain bars of gold and silver, copper, and all sorts of
goldsmiths' work, screens, varnished cabinets, porcelain,
tea, and other things. He sends sometimes one, two or three
[junks] to Tonkin, of two to three hundred tons at furthest,
with cloth, coral, tin, ivory, pepper, saltpetre, sappanwood
and some other commodities of the Indies, (and silver to
the value of one third of the capital,) for which he has
musk, lengths of silk, (raw and yellow silk, camlets,[1] several
kinds of satins, velvets, all kinds of) varnished wood,
(porcelains suitable for the Indies) and bars of gold. To
Macao the king sends one ship at the most, laden with the
same merchandise as for China. One may yet send there
haberdashery items, gold and silver lace, silk, and arms, for
which are received the same merchandise as in China, but
not at such a good rate.

In the kingdom of Laos the Siamese conduct trade both
overland and by river on flat boats. Cloth and linen of Surat
and the Coromandel coast are sent there, and the returns
are rubies, musk, gum, elephants' teeth, camphor, rhinoceros horns, buffalo and elk skins, and there is great profit
in this trade, because there's no risk to run.

To Cambodia the king sends small barks with a few
cloths, Surat and coastal linen, and kitchen utensils which

---

[1]   Costly Eastern fabrics.

come from China, for which he has brought him elephants' teeth, benjamin, three sorts of gutta gums, buffalo and elk skins, birds' nests for China, of which I shall speak hereafter, (and stag penises).

They sometimes send to Cochin-China, but seldom; for this people is untractable, being most of them unfaithful, which greatly hinders commerce with them. They carry, when they go, silver of Japan, to great profit, red laurel, yellow wax, rice, lead, saltpetre, some red and black cloths, some white linen, potter's clay, vermilion, and quicksilver.[1]

For which they have raw silk, candied and brown sugar, a little pepper, and birds' nests. These are made like those of swallows, found on rocks by the seaside; they are a good commodity for China, and several other places, for these nests, after being well-washed and dried, become as hard as horn, and they are put into broths. They are of admirable virtue to the sick and languishing persons, and to those who are troubled with pains in their stomach. Some of them have been brought into France.[2] [In addition, come] (eaglewood and allagoch, copper, and other merchandise, gold of several touchstones, and sappanwood.)

When there's no vessel to be had at freight,[3] they send one to Surat, laden with copper, tin, saltpetre, alum, elephants' teeth, sappanwood, and several other merchandises which come from other parts of India, and the returns

---

[1] Red laurel is possibly the cherry laurel; its leaves distilled in water contained a small quantity of prussic acid. Vermilion is another term for cinnabar, and quicksilver the old term for mercury.

[2] The two methods or preparing them are described, in very similar terms, by both Choisy and Tachard, during their return journey to France, the source of the information probably being one of the Siamese in the party of Kosa Pan travelling to France with the returning Chaumont mission.

[3] For hire, in order to transport merchandise.

are linen cloth and other European commodities, when there comes none to Siam.

They also trade with the coasts of Coromandel, Malabar, Bengal, and Tenasserim; the commodities are elephants, tin, saltpetre, copper, lead; and the returns are linen of all kinds.

There is seldom any trade to Borneo; this is an isle near that of Java, where the returns are pepper, dragons' blood, white camphor, yellow wax, eaglewood, pitch, gold, pearls, and the best diamonds in the world. (Taken there are merchandise from Surat, some lengths of red and green linen, and Spanish coin.) The prince that possesses this island barely tolerates trade, fearing always some surprise, and will suffer no European to settle in his countries. There have been some French merchants trading there, for he trusts them rather than any other nation.[1]

There is also a trade driven to Timor, an isle near the Moluccas, whence is drawn yellow and white wax, gold of three touchstones, slaves, (black gamouti [?] which is used for making ropes,) and thither is sent linen of Surat, lead, elephants' teeth, powder, eau-de-vie, some arms, red and black cloth, and silver. The people here are peaceable, and negotiate fairly. Here are a great many Portuguese.

As to the commodities produced in Siam, there is only tin, lead, sappanwood, ivory, skins of elks and elephants, areca, small pieces of iron, and a good quantity of rice. There will be a store of pepper in time, that is to say, next year. But you may find here commodities from all the places before-mentioned, and fairly cheap. Here are brought pieces of English cloth and serges, a little coral and amber, cloth from the Coromandel coast and Surat, money in paistres which are trucked.[2] But, as I now said, most

---

[1] Since there were several sultans ruling different parts of Borneo, Chaumont may be guilty of deluding his readers here.
[2] Bartered, exchanged.

merchants have left trading here since the king would turn merchant, (and foreigners now bring here very) few goods, for the ships that were wont to come here came not the last year, so that there's little to be found, all being in the king's and his ministers' hands, who sell for what they please.[1]

The kingdom of Siam is near three hundred leagues long, without reckoning the tributary kingdoms, to wit, Cambodia, Johor, Pattani, Kedah, etc.[2] (That is from the north to the south; it is narrower from east to west.) It's bounded northward by the kingdom of Pegu, and by the Sea of the Ganges on the side of the west, and from the south, by the little Strait of Malacca, which was taken from the King of Siam by the Portuguese, who had been masters of it more than sixty years. The Hollanders have taken it from them, and are the present masters of it.[3] On the east, it's bounded by the sea, and by the mountains which divide it from Cambodia and Laos.

The situation of the kingdom is advantageous for commerce, by reason of the great extent of its coasts, lying as it were between two seas, which open the passage to so many vast regions. Its coasts are five hundred leagues around, and are everywhere accessible, from Japan, China, the Philippine Islands, Tonkin, Cochin-China, Champa, Cambodia, Java, Sumatra, Golconda, Bengal, and from all

---

[1] The previous pages give one of the most complete acccounts of Siam's regional trade at the time, and the recent imposition of royal trading monopoly was an important factor in the decline of Ayutthaya as an entrepôt which began before the end of the reign of King Narai.

[2] Spelt 'Camboges, Gehor, Patavi, Queda'. The 'etc.' indicates either sloth or disinterest on Chaumont's part. Choisy adds Jambi, in northern Sumatra, to the list. It is interesting that Laos is not considered tributary.

[3] Malacca was occupied by the Portuguese from 1511 to 1641, and by the Dutch from the latter date.

the coasts of Coromandel, Persia, Surat, Mecca and the rest of Arabia, and Europe; and therefore the country is capable of a very great commerce, would the king permit all the foreign merchants to return and trade as heretofore.

The kingdom is divided into eleven provinces, to wit, that of Siam, Martaban, Tenasserim, Junk Ceylon [Phuket], Kedah, Perak, Johor, Pahang, Pattani, Ligor [Nakhon Si Thammarat], and Chaiya.[1] The provinces had heretofore the quality of kingdoms, but are all now under the sole power of the King of Siam, who sets governors over them.

There are some which may retain the name of principalities, but the governors depend on the king, and pay him tribute. Siam is the principal province of this kingdom: the capital city is situated 14 degrees and a half of latitude northward, and, as I have said, on the side of a great and stately river, and vessels laden come up to the gates of the city, which lies above forty leagues distant from the sea, and reaches above two hundred leagues up the country, and by this means it leads into part of the provinces which I have above mentioned.[2] This river abounds with fish, and its sides are well peopled, although they lie under water one part of the year. The earth is indifferently fruitful, but ill-dressed. The inundation proceeds from great rains, which fall for three or four

---

[1]   Given as 'Siam, Matavin, Tanaserin, Josalam, Reda, Pra, Ior, Paam, Parana, Ligor, and Siama'. This information appears to be lifted, without being updated, from Jacques de Bourges, *Relation du Voyage de Monsiegneur l'Evêque de Béryte... jusqu'au Royaume de Siam et autres lieux* (Paris, 1666). Choisy lists twelve provinces, only three of which are the same as those listed by Chaumont: Sri Ayutthaya, Bangkok, Phitsanulok, Phetchaburi, Phichai, Kamphengphet, Ratchaburi, Tenasserim, Ligor, Kanchanaburi, Nakhon Ratchasima, and Nakhon Sawan.

[2]   The Chao Phya River leads nowhere near the provinces listed by Chaumont, other than the capital, Siam, but does link some of those named by Choisy.

months together, which makes their rice grow apace, so that the longer the inundation lasts, the more rice they gather; and so far are they from complaining, that their greatest fear is of excessively dry weather. There are several lands [that] lie untilled for want of inhabitants, which has happened by the preceding wars, and the Siamese being enemies of labour, they love only those things that are easy; so that those abandoned plains and thick forests which are to be seen on the mountains serve for a retreat to elephants, tigers, wild boars and cows, deer, does, rhinoceros, and other animals, which are here in great quantities.

CHAPTER TEN

The produce of Siam

As to plants and fruits, there are many kinds in the country, but which are not rare and which cannot easily be brought over to France, by reason of the length of the sea journey. There are no birds but what we have in France, excepting one like a blackbird, which counterfeits the laughing of a man, his singing and whistling.[1]

The fruits the most esteemed are the durians; they have a very strong scent, which does not agree with everybody, but as to their taste, 'tis excellent. This fruit is very hot and dangerous to one's health if a man eats much of it. There is a great nut, about which is a kind of cream shut in a rind (surrounded by several spikes in the form of diamond points), which my palate could never approve of.

The mango is in this country in prodigious quantities, and this is the best fruit of the Indies, of an exquisite taste, no ways incommoding, unless a man eat too much of them, then indeed they may cause a fever. It has the shape of an almond, but is as big as a large pear. (Its skin is quite thin and the flesh is yellow.)

---

[1] The myna bird.

The mangosteen is a fruit like a green nut, which has within it a white fruit, of a sharp and pleasant taste, like that of a peach or plum; it's very cold, and yet stringent.

The jackfruit is a great fruit which is very good, but hot and indigestible, and causes fluxes in the bowels when one eats of it with excess.

The pineapple is almost like the durian, that is to say in respect of its skin. It has at its end a crown of leaves like the artichoke; its meat is very good, tasting like a peach and an apricot together; it's very hot and strong, which makes it commonly eaten soaked in wine.

The figs[1] are a sweet fruit of a kind nature, and healthful, yet somewhat flegmatic; there are of them all the year long.

The ate[2] is a very good sweet fruit, and does no hurt; there are who esteem it more than all the fruits in the Indies. There are oranges of all kinds, which are good too.

The papaya is a very good fruit, but the tree which bears it lives only two years.

The grapefruit is a wholesome fruit which is like the orange, but of a sharper taste. There are several other fruits which are not so good.[3]

They began some years past to sow much corn in the high lands near the mountains, which comes up well, and is very good. As also vines which have been several times planted, but they grow and do not last, being eaten up to the roots by a sort of white ant.

---

[1] Bananas, which he obviously found dull.

[2] Possibly the guava, which La Loubère's English translator calls by its Frenchified term, 'goyaye' (*gouvaie*), then called in Siamese *luk-kiac*, now *farang* (or in the north-east *sida*).

[3] La Loubère also discusses, in addition to the guava and the pomelo, the plum-like moussida, the 'ox-heart' (rambutan), the tamarind, and the coconut.

There are a great many sugarcanes which yield in abundance, as also tobacco, which the Siamese eat with areca and lime.

As to the areca, the Siamese esteem this fruit more than any other, for this is their common food. There is such a great quantity of it, that the markets are full of it; and a Siamese would think himself guilty of a great indecency should he speak to anyone without having his mouth full of areca, betel, lime, or tobacco.

(There is a great quantity of rice throughout the kingdom, and very cheap too, as this country is always flooded, making it more abundant. For the rice is raised in water, and as the water rises, so the rice grows in tandem. If the water rises one foot in twenty-four hours, the rice grows in proportion and ever has its stem above the water. It stays only five or six months in the land, and comes like oats.)

CHAPTER ELEVEN

The capital, people, the king's routine and family

There is no city in the East where is seen more different nations than in the capital city of Siam, and where so many different tongues are spoken. It is two leagues round, and half a league broad, well peopled, although so much under water that it resembles rather an island (than a city on solid ground). There are none but the Moors, Chinese, the French and the English who dwell in the town, all the other nations being lodged round about it in camps, each nation by themselves, who, should they come all of them into one body, would take up as much room as the town which was formerly so commercial, but the reasons I before mentioned hinder most foreign nations to come and bring anything with them.

The people, as before mentioned, are obliged to serve the king four months in the year, and longer if he needs them; he gives them no pay, they being obliged to keep themselves, and therefore the women work to feed their husbands[1]. As to the officers, from the greatest lords of the court to the meanest of the kingdom, the king only allows them some very small gratifications, being as much slaves

---

[1] This contradicts what he said earlier about the king providing rice and the men having to work half the year.

as the rest, and this saves him a great deal of money. As to the distant provinces whose inhabitants do not actually serve, each singular person pays him a certain head tax.

I arrived at a time when the country was wholly under water, the town seemed the more pleasant for it. The streets are very long, broad, and straight, there are on both hands houses built on piles, and trees planted round about them, which makes for admirable verdure, and you cannot go to them but in a boat. You would think to see at one glance a city, a sea, and a vast forest, where are several pagodas, which are their churches, most of which are much gilded. About these pagodas there are places like churchyards, planted with trees, which are for the most part fruit trees. The houses of the Talapoins are the biggest and finest in the town, and are exceedingly numerous.

The country is wholsomer than any of the Indies; the Siamese are commonly well shaped, although all of them have tanned countenances; they are fairly tall, their hair is black and they wear it short by reason of the heat, they bathe often, which contributes to the preservation of their health; the Europeans who dwell there do the same. They hold their markets during the inundations in special areas and in their barges.

The king rises in the morning, and holds a great council about ten of the clock, wherein all affairs are treated of, and which lasts until midday. This being ended, his physicians assemble to know the state of his health, and he afterwards goes to dinner; he makes but one real meal a day. After dinner he withdraws into his apartment, where he sleeps two or three hours, and 'tis not known about what he employs himself the rest of the day, it not being permitted, not even to his officers, to enter into his chamber. About ten at night he holds another privy council, where there are seven or eight mandarins of those which are most in his favour; which council last till midnight. Afterwards he has histories or verses made after their manner read to him, to divert him, and commonly after this council, Mr Constance tarries with him alone, to whom he opens his whole mind; the king being sensible of his vast parts, his conversation pleases him, (and he communicates all his most secret thoughts); he ordinarily only withdraws at three after midnight to go to sleep. This is the daily manner of the king's living (and in this way all the affairs of the kingdom come before him). At certain times he takes pleasure in hunting, as I already observed. (He is very fond of jewels, even those of enamel and glass.) He is always very neatly dressed.

He has no other children but a daughter, who is called the Princess Queen[1] of twenty-seven or twenty-eight years of age. The king greatly loves her. I was told she was a handsome woman, but she has never been seen by any men, she eats in the same place and at the same time her father does, but at a table apart, and she is served by women, who are always prostrate in her presence.

This princess has her court consisting of mandarins' ladies, who see her every day; and she holds a council with her women about her own affairs. She distributes justice to those belonging to her about all her affairs. The king having given her provinces, she maintains her court with the revenue, and conducts her own justice. It has happened sometimes that when her women have been proved guilty of great slanders, or revealing secrets of great importance, she has made their mouths be sewed up.

Before the death of the queen her mother, she was as 'tis said inclinable to great severities, (but since she has lost her,

[1]   Krom Luang Yothathep, the only child of Narai, by his sister and queen Sri Chulalok, who died about 1680. Yothathep was forced to marry Narai's usurper, Petracha. Western visitors, none of whom ever saw her, were fascinated by her.

she behaves with much greater gentleness.) She does sometimes go ahunting with the king, but 'tis in a very fine chair placed on an elephant, and where though she is not seen, yet she beholds all that passes. There are horsemen who march before her to clear the way, and if there be anyone in the road that cannot soon get out, he prostrates himself on the ground and turns his back towards her. She is all day shut up with her women, diverting herself with no needlework. Her dress is plain and very light, her legs bare, she had light pumps on her feet (without heels, in a different fashion from those of France. That which serves her as a skirt is a piece of silk or cotton called a pagne,[1] which covers her from the waist to below, both ends being joined, but without folds; from above the waist she has only a muslin blouse which falls over her form of skirt, and which is made in the same manner as that of the men. She has a scarf on her bosom which covers her neck and passes over her arms.) She is always bare-headed, and wears her hair not passing four or five fingers long, (which makes her head appear as of a newly born.) She is a great lover of sweet scents, anointing her head with oil; for in those countries their hair must look shining to be fine. She bathes every day, (even more than once,) which is the custom of all Indians, as well men as women. I have learnt all this of Madame Constance,[2] who oft makes her court to her. All

---

[1] So called by the French, from the Spanish *paño*, a length of cloth from the waist to the knees.

[2] Phaulkon was converted to Catholicism in 1682 by two Jesuits, Maldonado and Thomas. To ensure a return to a virtuous path, he needed a wife, and was duly married soon after to the devout Maria Guyomar de Pinha, whose father was of Bengali and Japanese extraction, and whose mother of Portuguese-Japanese descent (and who may have been free with her favours). 'Madame Constance' was apparently the only non-Siamese admitted to the court of the Princess Queen.

the women which are in her chamber are always prostrate with their faces on the ground in rank order; that is to say, the ancientest are nearest her. They have the liberty to look on the princess, which men have not in reference to the king, be they of what quality they will; for as long as they are in his presence, they lie prostrate on the ground, even when they speak to him.

The king has two brothers,[1] who according to Siamese custom have the right to succeed to the crown in preference to his children.

When he goes out to hunt or walk, notice is given to all Europeans not to be in the way, unless they will lie prostrate on the ground. A while before he goes out of his palace you hear the warning trumpets sound and drums beat, and who march before the king. At this noise soldiers who stand in a row prostrate themselves, their foreheads to the ground, with their muskets under them. They are in this posture as long as the king can see them on his elephant, where he is placed on a covered gilt chair. The horse guards which attend him, which consist of Moors, is about forty (cavalry troopers trotting on his sides). All the king's household are on foot in front, behind and on either side, holding their hands closed.[2]

There are some of the principal mandarins who follow him on elephants, ten or twelve officers who carry great

---

[1]   They were in fact half-brothers. The elder, Chao Fa Aphaitot, was deformed, and partly paralyzed, hot-tempered and often drunk. The younger, Chao Fa Noi, was comely but in 1683 the victim of an intrigue of Petracha, who was permitted by Narai to beat him in punishment so severely that he lost the use of his tongue, which some said was a diplomatic indisposition. They were held, with little evidence, to be embroiled in the Makassar rebellion of 1686, and both were put to death by Petracha on 9 July 1688, one or two days before the death of Narai himself.

[2]   That is, joined and raised as in prayer.

umbrellas about the king, and it is only these who do not prostrate themselves. (For as soon as the king halts, although) all the others fall down on their faces, those that are on the elephants only bend down.

CHAPTER TWELVE

The manner of receiving ambassadors

As to the manner which the King of Siam observes in the reception of ambassadors, as those of Tonkin, Cochin-China, Golconda, Malaya, Java, and other kings, he receives them in a great hall covered with carpets, the nobles and chief men of the kingdom being in another hall which stands lower than the former, all of them prostrate on carpets in expectation of the king's appearance at a window which is over against them. The hall wherein the ambassador must be is raised about ten or twelve feet, and distant from this hall where the king should be thirty feet. 'Tis known the king is upon appearing by the noise of trumpets, drums and other instruments. The ambassador is behind a wall which encloses this room in expectation of the king's coming, and the ministers' orders, which the king sends by one of the officers of his chamber, according to the quality of ambassador, (for his officers serve on such occasions.) After the ministers have the king's permission, the door of the hall is opened, and thence the ambassador appears with his interpreters, and the officer of the king's chamber who serves as master of ceremonies walks before them (and prostrates himself three times on the carpet, lowering his head in their manner, even though the master of cermonies) proceeds on his knees, with his hands closed.

The ambassador with his interpreters follows him in the same posture, with great modesty, till he is come one half of the way where he is to go, and then bows himself three times in the same manner. He continues walking to the corner nearest where the nobles are, and then he begins to bow again. There he stops; there is a table between the king and the ambassador, about eight foot distant, where lie the presents which the ambassador brings the king, and between this table and the ambassador there is a mandarin who receives the king's words. In this hall are the king's ministers, distant from the ambassador about three paces, and the captain of the people whence the ambassador is, between him and the minister.

The king begins to speak first, and not the ambassador, ordering his minister to enquire of the ambassador when he departed from the presence of the king his master, whether the king and all the royal family be in good health, to which the ambassador answers what's fitting through his interpreter. The interpreter tells it to the captain of the nation[1] of which the ambassador is, the captain to the Barcalon, and the Barcalon to the king. After this the king offers some questions about two or three points concerning the embassy; then the king orders the officer close to the table to give betel to the ambassador, which is the sign to present him a vest. Immediately the king retires with the noise of drums and trumpets, and other instruments. The ambassador's first audience passes between him and the minister, who examines the letter, and the presents of the prince who has sent them. The ambassador does not present the letter to the king, but to the minister, after some days of council held on this subject.

When they be ambassadors of independent rulers of Oriental kingdoms, as of the countries of Persia, the Great

---

[1] The head of the resident colony from a particular country.

Mogul,[1] the Emperor of China or Japan, they are received in this following manner.

The grandees of the first and second rank go to the foot of the window where the king is, to prostrate themselves according to their qualities on the carpets, when those of the third, fourth, and fifth rank are in a lower hall, and expect the king's coming, who appears at a window which is inserted into a wall, and is raised ten foot. The ambassadors are in a place out of the palace, expecting the master of ceremonies, who comes and receives them, and there are the same ceremonies used which I have already mentioned. The ambassador entering into the palace puts his hands upon his head,[2] and after marching through two halls climbs the stairs, which are opposite the window where the king is, and when he is at the top, he claps one knee to the ground. Then immediately a door is opened that he may appear before the king, and the same ceremonies are practiced which I have already mentioned. There is a golden platter on the table wherein lies the letter which the ambassador brought, translated and open, having been received by the ministers some days before in a hall appointed for that purpose. When the ambassador is in his place, the minister's deputy takes the letter, and reads it aloud; which done, the king asks the ambassador some questions by his minister, his minister by the captain of the nation, and the captain by the interpreter, (and the interpreter finally speaks to the ambassador. These questions enquire if the king his master and the royal family are in good health, and if the ambassador is charged with any matter other than that in the letter; to which the ambassador replies as the case needs be. The king asks him

---

1   As noted earlier, Aurangzeb (r.1658-1707), whose conquests in India saw the peak of Mogul expansion.
2   Not 'upon' but 'to', giving the traditional *wai* of respect.

three or four more questions, and gives order that he be given a vest and some betel, after which he retires to the sound of drums and trumpets. Those who have received him lead him back to his lodging without other company.)

Having learnt this manner of receiving ambassadors, which did not seem agreeable to the greatness of the monarch by whom I was sent, I desired two mandarins who attended me by the king's order to inform him that I entreated him I might have the same reception which ambassadors are wont to have in France, which was granted me in the manner related.[1]

---

[1] It was granted verbally without being implemented, as the text shows, though Chaumont was allowed a chair to sit on.

A Chinese 'comedy' such as Chaumont and Choisy saw on 1 November 1685.

PART III

Siamese theatre presented to the French ambassadors by Phaulkon on the occasion of the accession to the throne of the King of Portugal.

CHAPTER THIRTEEN

From Siam to the Cape

Having given some small account of the religion, customs, government, situation and divers curious things concerning the kingdom of Siam, I now return to relate my departure from the roads, where I interrupted the narrative of my account, and which was on the 22nd of December, 1685.

We hoisted sail at three of the morning[1] with a good northern wind, which continued all along the coasts of Cambodia, which is a kingdom adjoining to that of Siam, and going towards Cochin-China. The peoples of these two kingdoms have the same belief, and live after the same manner. There passed nothing remarkable to the Strait of Bangka, where I ran on ground, opposite an isle called Lucapara, on a muddy bank where there were but three fathoms of water, and our vessel required above sixteen feet. This did not much disturb me, though it did much the ship's crew, whom I sent to sound about the vessel, and more depth was found. I caused a small anchor to be brought, to which there was a cable, and we got off this bank using the ship's capstans in less than five hours.[2]

[1] Choisy says it was 2 a.m.
[2] This occurred on 7 January 1686. Choisy notes it was almost in the same spot that the vessel ran aground on the outward journey, on 29 August 1685.

Though I had a good Dutch pilot, yet I caused this strait to be often sounded, both going and coming.

I continued my course and arrived at Bantam the 11th of January, 1686. As soon as I had cast anchor there, I sent Mr de Sibois,[1] my officer, to compliment the governor, and to have fresh provisions. He sent me for a present six oxen, fruits and herbs. (I took on no water, because it is very difficult to obtain,) and I remained in this road but thirty hours. We weighed anchor on the 12th at night, but the calm overtook us, which obliged us to cast anchor.

On the 13th I weighed anchor, and we had all that day calms and contrary winds, but at night there arose a small wind which made us double the point of Bantam, and pass the Strait of Sunda in less than eight hours: I was obliged to hove to opposite Prince's Isle, which is at the mouth of the strait, in expectation of the frigate *Maligne,* which could not follow us, but at length joined us.

On the 14th I held my course directly for the Cape of Good Hope with a favourable north wind, and north-north-east. The 23rd at break of day, having made about an hundred and fifty leagues, we saw the Isles of Holy Cross,[2] which surprised us, because the evening before I caused the pilots' point to be showed us, who all said we were at more than fifteen leagues of latitude southward, and twenty of longitude, from them.

These lands lie very low, and had it been three or four hours in the night we had certainly run on ground, but it pleased God to preserve us. We attributed this error to the tides which ran against us (and prevented us from going as far ahead as we thought); we passed these isles quickly, the wind blowing hard, and continued our course. The sea was

---

[1] Sibois served as adjutant on the return journey, Forbin having been left (against his will) in Siam, to train the king's troops.

[2] The Cocos Islands, so called by Choisy.

full of fish in these parts, and there are a great many birds; the weather was fair, and we every day made thirty, forty, fifty, or sixty leagues with a following wind. We were diverted by a pleasant game we saw carried on by the albacores and bonitos,[1] and a small fish called a flying fish, who, when he sees himself pursued by fish whose food he is, jumps out of the water, and flies as long as his wings are moist, which may be as far perhaps as the flight of a quail. But there is a bird called a strawtail, which has this name on account of a great feather in its tail, longer than the others by more than half a foot, and which has the form and almost the colour of a straw; he is always in the air, and when he sees this flying fish leave the water, he lets himself fall down upon it, as a bird of prey on his game, and sometimes goes deep into the water after it; so that the flying fish seldom fails being taken.

On the 15th of February, we found ourselves not far from the Isle of Maurice,[2] where we suddenly met with a blast of wind that lasted us three days. The sea was extremely rough, and gave us a great deal of trouble, the waves passing oft over our ship, which made us to ply our pumps often to clear it of water.

On the 19th the weather grew fair, and gave us leisure to set to rights what the sea had disordered; (there were great nails protruding from the planking holding the stern-frame beneath the casing, and this was caused by the waves breaking on the vessel as against a rock.) The first night wherein this bad weather happened, the frigate that was with me left us, the rendez-vous being at the Cape of Good Hope. Keeping on our course we had two more blasts of hard weather, which much incommoded us, (for the sea was extremely rough, the winds almost throughout turning

[1]   Kinds of tunny.
[2]   Mauritius.

119

in every direction of the compass), in such a manner that the waves beat against each other, causing any ship to suffer greatly.

On the 10th of March, about two hours after noon, we perceived a vessel. At first I thought it was that which had left me, but coming nearer, we saw her carrying English colours, and being willing to hear news, and supposing she came from Europe, I came up to her, and when I was near sent out my longboat with an officer on board to know if there were any wars, for when a man has been long away from France, one knows not whom to trust, especially when one has to anchor at foreign places. Word was brought me 'twas an English merchantman, who had departed from London five months since, and had touched nowhere, and that she intended straight for Tonkin, that the captain had told him that there was no war in France, and that all Europe was at peace; but yet there had been some revolt in England occasioned by the Duke of Monmouth, who had placed himself at the head of ten or twelve thousand men, but that the king's troops had routed them, and taken him prisoner; and that he was beheaded, and several of the persons taken with him were hanged, and so this rebellion was ended before he left.[1] He also told us that he had seen land the day before seven leagues off, which made us judge that we were thirty or thirty-five leagues off of it.

We held on our course the rest of the day and night, and the next morning at ten of the clock we spied land, seven or eight leagues windward of us. I sounded and we found fourscore fathom (which gave us to understand that it was land, and the Agulhas Bank; furthermore there was a great

---

[1]   James Scott, Duke of Monmouth (1649-1685), was a natural son of Charles II, and led a Protestant revolt against James II after his accession to the throne in 1685, which was put down in the manner described.

number of birds. This bank is thirty leagues broad and the same in length, and bottom can be sounded six score fathom upward). We clapped on all our sail to endeavour to get before night to the Cape of Good Hope. The next morning at break of day we saw it and doubled it; about ten of the clock we espied a vessel windward of us, and drawing near we found 'twas the frigate, which as I have said left us near the Isle of Maurice. This was the second time after a lengthy separation we came both together the same day as our arrival, which seldom happens on a long sea journey. When I was ready to cast anchor, the wind blew so hard against us that I was forced to tack about and anchor at the Isle of Robben, which is about three leagues from the fort of the Cape.

CHAPTER FOURTEEN

Dutch policies and explorations at the Cape

The next morning being the 13th of March we weighed anchor, and went to anchor near the fort, were I arrived about two of the clock. I found there nine vessels which came from Batavia, and were bound for Europe. I sent the Chevalier de Sibois to compliment the governor, and to ask his leave to send eight or ten sick people on shore, and take in fresh water and necessary provisions. He received respectfully my compliment, and bid the officer tell me I was master, and that I might do what I pleased. Arriving therein at the time of their autumn, wherein all fruits are good, he sent me melons, grapes, and salads. I saluted the fort with seven cannon; for the king's order is to salute the forts first, and they were exactly answered. The vessel which carried the admiral's flag saluted me afterwards with seven pieces, and I returned him with the same. There were in this fleet three flagships, to wit, the admiral, vice-admiral, and counter-admiral. The fruits sent me were excellent good, as well as the salads; the melons were very fine, and the grapes better than those in France. I went to walk in their fine garden, about which I have already written, and which made me remember those in France. The great quantity of vegetables growing there gave much pleasure to our crews, for the governor gave us as much as we pleased. (There are in that place a great many quinces which are very good for travellers, for ordinarily the illnesses arising from these [sea] passages are fluxes of the blood.)

The governor is a man of sense, very appropriate for the colonies, and 'tis said, if he remains long there, he will make a fine settlement in those parts. When there be any Hollanders that will dwell there, he gives them as much land as they will, builds them a house, gives them oxen for tillage, and all other cattle and utensils that are necessary; all of which is valued, and when they are able, they pay the Company for them. They are obliged to sell all the fruits of their lands to the Company, at a certain price, which is advantageous to both parties. The wine that they buy of them for sixteen crowns an hogshead, they sell for an hundred to foreigners and to their own fleets which pass this way; that is to say, to the seamen who drink it on the spot. Sheep, oxen and other things are sold in proportion, which brings a great revenue to the Company, and makes their fleets refresh themselves at small charge, and remain months (and periods of six weeks together) there, according to the number of sick persons they bring.

When I arrived, 'twas not long since the governor was returned from a discovery which he had made of gold and silver mines; (he brought back thence several nuggets.) 'Tis said that in these mines there is much gold and silver, and that they are easily worked, being shallow. He went up to two hundred and fifty leagues into the country. He carried along with him three or four Hottentots from the Cape, who spoke Dutch, who led him to the next nation, which was likewise Hottentot, and took others in his way. He met with near nine different nations, and as he changed each tribe he took some of the new ones along with him, to make himself understood. He has, I am told, gotten great light in what he aimed at. He says the last nation is the most polished, and that they came before him, men, women and children, dancing, being all clothed with the skins of tigers, of which they make great robes which hang down to their feet. He brought one of these Hottentots, whom he causes to be taught Dutch, to return thither next year. All these several peoples have many cattle, and this is their revenue. The governor had with him fifty soldiers, a painter to draw colours of animals, birds, serpents and such plants as he should find; a draughtsman to mark the course they took, and a pilot, for they always went by the compass, and drove along with them three hundred oxen, to carry their provisions, and draw fourteen or fifteen carts. When they met with any mountains they dismounted their carriages, and took out whatsoever was therein, and loaded the oxen with it, and thus passed over them. Being advanced in the country, they were three or four days before the could find any water, which much incommoded them. He was five and an half months in this journey.

He met with several wild beasts, and says that the elephants are monstrous, far exceeding in bigness those of the Indies; as also rhinoceros of a prodigious size. He saw one with which he thought he should have been killed; for when this animal is in a fury, there is no weapon can stop him. His skin is hard, and musket shots are nothing to it. (They have to be taken above the shoulder to be killed.) They have two horns; (I brought back three,) two of which grow together in the skin of this animal.

The abode I made at the Cape furnished me with fish during the time of Lent, in which we were. I saw a whale of astonishing size; it came within half a pistol shot of our vessel. There were also birds in quantity, which gave us the same diversion as those strawtails of which I have spoken.[1]

[1] The 1687 translation here details several pages of directions taken and leagues covered on a daily basis from leaving Siam to arriving at the Cape.

CHAPTER FIFTEEN

From the Cape to Brest, and those on board

On the 26th of March at two in the afternoon, I set sail with a good wind. In leaving the bay near the Dutch fort of the Cape of Good Hope, I saw three vessels who made towards the Cape, but I could not distinguish of what nation they were. I believe them to have been Dutch, because this number was expected from the Isle of Ceylon.[1] After we had passed forty leagues from thence, we found the sea very boisterous, which gave us much trouble, but we continued on our course to pass the Line in the same longitude as we did when going.

Our voyage must needs be pleasant for, as I already noted, the King of Siam, sent with us ambassadors into France, to show the king how earnestly he desired his friendship; his great qualities and renown having long since made considerable report in the Indies. He told me in an audience that he would give them no instructions on the ceremonial of France, even though it was very different from his kingdom's, because he was persuaded the king would not require anything of them prejudicial to his interests, and that he charged me to counsel them what

---

[1]   The Dutch evicted the Portuguese from Ceylon (Sri Lanka) in 1658.

they had to do for the best when they came to France, being sure that I would not impose upon them.

We had then with us three ambassadors, the most considerable persons in Siam. The first, (named Ok-phra Wisut Sunthorn)[1] is brother to the late deceased Barcalon, who was the king's chief minister, a man of sense, having ever been close to his brother, playing an important role in all matters during his period in office. This person came to receive me at the mouth of the River of Siam when I arrived, and has been ever with me, attending me wherever I went. The first time I saw him he seemed to me an upright person, free from all affectation and reservedness, which made me tell Mr Constance that he would be a very fit man to be sent over ambassador to France.

The second of the ambassadors is (called Ok-luang Kanlaya Ratchamaitri,[2] and is) very aged, and wants not wit, having been ambassador in China, and acquitted himself to the king his master's satisfaction. The third, (named Ok-khun Siwisan Wacha,[3]) is aged about twenty-five or thirty years, and his father is ambassador in Portugal.

These three gentlemen are very gentle, obliging, and good-natured, and have a very equable disposition. They write down the smallest matters they see; I imagine they will be much occupied in France, where they will encounter so many things worthy of their admiration; neither do I doubt but they will give a true account of them to the king their master.

---

[1] The 1687 translation did not name him. He was more generally known as Kosa Pan and was to be the toast of French society in the coming months. His elder brother was a former *Phra Klang*, Chao Phya Kosathipodi.

[2] Chaumont gives an additional name for him: 'Ockhun Arucha Ratsa'.

[3] Chaumont gives an unrecognizable form of his name 'Ockhun Jurin Ocman Viset Ppubaan'.

They should have had twelve mandarins for their retinue, but they have but eight, four of them being left behind at Siam, because they came not soon enough on board. They brought with them twelve small boys to learn the tongue and trades, but some of them are also left behind with the four mandarins (who were not able to join us, along with some of the ambassadors' domestics, though a score remain with them.)

(They have a great quantity of fine presents for the king, the dauphin, the dukes of Burgundy and Anjou, and also have some for the marquises de Seignelay and Colbert de Croissy.[1] Among these presents are many gold and silver vases, Japan and Manila works, a great quantity of very rare porcelain, screens from China and Japan, many jewels from all parts of the Indies, cabinets, chests, varnished writing desks embellished with silver, vases of incised terracotta which are as light as feathers, two small golden boats, one for the king and one for the Duke of Burgundy, two cannons for the king, about two or three pounds of cannon balls of cold-beaten iron, decorated with silver like inlaid pieces, rhinoceros horns, bezoar stones, and many other things which I do not remember. These presents are extremely valuable, and the King of Siam was pleased to send into France all that he had which was most rare.)

The Abbé de Lionne was entreated by this king to go to France with his ambassadors (being persuaded he could be of great help to them) because he speaks their language (and is a most upright person of great piety). The king also told Mr Le Vachet that he would be very glad that he

---

[1]   Jean-Baptiste Colbert (1651-1690), Marquis de Seignelay, was the son of the minister Colbert (1619-1683) and at the time Secretary of State for the Navy. Charles-François Colbert (1626-1696), Marquis de Croissy, younger brother of Colbert and so uncle of Seignelay, was Secretary of State for Foreign Affairs.

would return with his ambassadors, being able to be equally useful to them, as he is an active person. We have also with us the Abbé de Choisy, who went to Siam to reside there in quality of ambassador, in case the king should become a Christian;[1] he is a very honest gentleman with much wit and merit. (He took his orders in that country and) said his first mass on board our vessel;[2] his good example and his sermons were very edifying for us. The Abbé de Chayla[3] was of our company, an able man who often preached to us.

(I had as almoner the Abbé de Jully, with whom I was mighty pleased, as he gave us very fine sermons, and the ship's almoner, Mr Le Dot, took good care of all the crew. There was never a Sunday nor a feast day but that we had sermons, and I can say, thanks to God, that we lived on board ship with much piety with the help of all these gentlemen, who often exhorted those in the crew to live like true and faithful Christians; so that there were none who did not confess and frequently perform their devotions, which doubtless brought us the blessings of God for the duration of such a long sea voyage which could not have been more happily conducted.)

Mr de Vaudricourt[4] was in command of the *Oiseau*; he is a most excellent gentleman, one of the best and most

---

[1]   Chaumont, in saying this, is admitting the partial failure of his admittedly impossible mission.

[2]   Choisy took orders on 10 December 1685 in Lopburi at the hands of Louis Laneau, Bishop of Metellopolis; he preached his first sermon on board the *Oiseau* on 3 March 1686.

[3]   François de Langlade, Abbé de Chayla, was an independent traveller who was to be massacred by Protestants in the Cévennes in 1702.

[4]   Vaudricourt, who, with Joyeux, captain of the *Maligne*, was presented to King Narai at Lopburi (see Chapter Four), was made captain in 1673, and was to go again to Siam in 1687 with the La Loubère-Céberet mission as commander of the *Gaillard*.

careful seafaring men whom the king has in his service. I have much cause to praise him for the great care he took of everything concerning the vessel (where nothing was lacking thanks to the just precautions he took before our departure. It is difficult to believe this could have happened thus during such a long voyage).

(We also had Mr de Coriton, [with the rank of] captain of a light frigate, who is a very good officer, very careful and assiduous in his post.[1] We had as lieutenant the Chevalier de Forbin, whom I left with the King of Siam, and the Chevalier de Sibois, both very good officers, and for ensign Mr de Chammoreau,[2] who well knows his calling for the application he gives to it, and he is capable to being more than an ensign.)

(The king had accorded me the honour of twelve officers and marine guards to accompany me in my embassy. They were Messers de Francine, ensign, Saint Villiers, ensign, de Compiegne, de Fretteville, de Benneville, du Fay, de Joncoux,[3] Palu, La Forest, d'Herbouville, who died in the frigate en route, and Mr du Tertre, lieutenant on the frigate *Maligne*, who is a very honest man and a good officer. Mr de Joyeux[4] commanded that frigate and I have every possible reason to praise his conduct. I must also render this justice to all these gentlemen who were most prudent and in all respects corresponded to the choice His Majesty had made in selecting them. They

---

[1] Coriton was first officer on the *Oiseau*.

[2] Chammoreau went on the Duquesne-Guiton expedition to the East Indies in 1690-91 in command of the *Lion*.

[3] Fretteville and Joncoux went again to Siam with La Loubère in 1687. In one French edition of Chaumont, Benneville is spelt 'Seneville'.

[4] Joyeux went again to Siam in 1687 in command of the *Loire*, and took part in the Duquesne-Guiton expedition in 1690-91 in command of the *Florissant*.

studied navigation and mathematics with a teacher who remained in Siam when going, and on the return Father Tachard consented to assist them. Those who are not yet officers are capable of being so, and those that are [already] are capable of rising to the highest ranks. There was another marine guard who was ordered to accompany me to Siam with these gentlemen of whom I have just spoken, but he remained in France.[1] I can say in favour of the Chevalier du Fay that he is well capable of being promoted ensign, for he showed great application to learn the manoeuvres and all other matters concerning navigation.[2])

(I had as secretary the Sieur de La Brosse-Bonneau, who is a very honest person. Mr Constance indicated to me that he would be most obliged to have two of my trumpeters and my upholsterer. I left them with him with their agreement, and he promised them good wages. My butler asked me if he could remain there to negotiate some silver he had,[3] one of my lackeys remained with the head of the French [Indies] Company, and another remained with the Bishop of Metellopolis. The Abbé de Choisy also left two of his men there: one remained with Mr Constance, who promised to do something for him; I think he will place him in the navy. So that of the Frenchmen who went with me to Siam, some twelve or fifteen remained there in the service of the king or his minister.)

---

[1] Chaumont, who only lists eleven persons at the beginning of this paragraph, says, in Chapter Three, that he presented twelve attendant gentlemen to King Narai at his first audience. Forbin and Sibois probably made up the number to twelve, d'Herbouville having died.

[2] Chaumont does not mention in singling out du Fay for special praise that he was his nephew.

[3] The Sieur de Billy, who was promoted to be governor of Phuket, but ended up in prison in Ayutthaya in 1688 after the May coup, along with many other Frenchmen.

I continued my course still with a rear wind and I came near to the Isle of St Helena[1] which is inhabited by the English; such ships as come from the Indies touch there, that is to say when they go not to the Cape of Good Hope. I was told it was a very good and fruitful island. It lies sixteen degrees latitude southward. I passed the 19th of April in sight of the Isle of Ascension,[2] which is eight degrees southward of the Line. The isle is not inhabited; most vessels make some stay here to take tortoises, there being here great numbers of them, and they are no small refreshment to seafaring men. They live a month or six weeks without eating; they can only be taken at nights, for in the daytime they keep to the sea, and at night come to land to lay their eggs, which they hide in the sand. To take them you must lie hid with a great stick in your hand, surprise them when they come out of the water, and throw them on their backs so that they cannot stir. A man may strike fourscore or an hundred in a night (and by day they are loaded onto the vessels where they are kept on their backs). Here vessels come on purpose to take these animals and salt them, and then carry them to the isles of America, being bought by the inhabitants for their slaves.

Having a good wind I tarried not at all here, not being willing to lose time in such favourable weather in passing the equinoctial line; for sometimes a man is forced to be long about it by reason of calms and rains to be met there. The 28th of April I again passed the Line with admirable weather, the heats in no wise incommoding us. This is the fourth time I passed it on this journey without leaving my lined cloth justaucorp. All our men were in good health

---

[1] St Helena was ceded by the Dutch to the English and from 1659 was held under charter by the East India Company.

[2] Ascension Island was discovered by the Portuguese João de Nova in 1501; it passed to Britain in 1815 and was only inhabited from this date.

excepting four or five, who were sick of the gripes, which distemper they brought from Siam. This distemper is seldom cured in that country, and I lost about ten or twelve sailors or soldiers who died of it. We saw but few fish all along, which is unusual, for most often there are very many. We harpooned one called a blower, about eight foot long and four foot broad. He had a hole on the top of his head, through which he breathes, and throws up water into the air like a fountain. He made a great noise, and weighed about three hundredweight; he is good to eat. (The harpoon which is used to take it is like the iron tip of an arrow; when it enters, it cannot come out. The harpoon is attached to a fairly long piece of wood, to which is tied a rope. An adroit sailor holds the harpoon in his hand at the bows of the ship, and throws it at the fish when it comes close to him. Having pierced it, he reels out the rope so that the fish loses its blood and strength; then it is drawn into the vessel.) On the 29th we took two more fish in the same manner (which are called porpoises. They look very similar to the blower, except that their head and snout are long, and the blowers' are almost round.) They weighed about an hundred and fifty pounds a piece. (They are very good to eat.) I was but thirty-two days coming from the Cape of Good Hope to the Line, (whereas going I had taken seven weeks from the Line to the Cape, because the route is much longer when one has to seek out the west winds.)

On the 16th of May about midnight, we passed the Tropic of Cancer, according to the best judgment our pilots could make in taking the height. This was (thanks to God) the sixth time we passed the tropics in this voyage (having passed four times that of Capricorn); on leaving the torrid zone we entered the temperate with the benefit of a good wind.

The 1st of June we saw land, when we thought we were above an hundred and fifty leagues off it; this surprised us.

Because there arose great mists we were obliged to draw near it, and the weather clearing, we found it was the Isle of Flores, which is one of the Azores, and which lies most westward; it stands very high and there falls from its mountains great watercourses into the sea. (It was by this that we recognized it; we had doubtless found) currents to carry us to the west, when we made for above an hundred and fifty leagues eastward. The 5th we saw a vessel that came near us, but it being night we knew not what she was. On the 7th we saw another which advanced close to us. I sent an officer on board in my longboat, who brought me word it was an English vessel that came from Virginia and was bound to London; she was laden with tobacco. There being a great wind, and we outsailing her, soon left her behind. We had variable weather till the 12th, but about six of the clock at night, having a western rear wind, the sea grew so boisterous, it blowing hard also, that we were forced (the following day at ten of the clock in the morning) to hove to, though my pilots estimated we were within an hundred leagues distant from Brest. The weather being very cloudy because of the showers, and being afeared of coming close to land in such weather, for these blasts of winds last sometimes eight days together, (this obliged me once more to hove to) about ten of the clock at night on the 13th. The wind grew calm, and we again set sail, and on the 18th of June arrived (thanks be to God) in the road of Brest at four in the afternoon, where as soon as we had cast anchor I made both our ships fire their guns to salute the ambassadors of Siam, which I brought along with me to France.[1]

---

[1]   Again the 1687 translation at this point has several pages of directions and leagues covered from the Cape to Brest.

The audience chamber at Lopburi

PART IV

French gentlemen in the embassy in front of the palace gate at Lopburi

CHAPTER SIXTEEN

Presents brought from Siam

Memorandum of the King of Siam's presents to the King of France[1]

Two pieces of cast iron cannon six foot long, hammered cold, set out with silver, mounted on their carriages, garnished also with silver, made at Siam.

An ewer and basin of tambac, a metal more esteemed than gold, which is made at Siam after the country's fashion.

A golden ewer embossed on four fronts, with a flat basin for its support, made at Japan.

A golden ship, called a junk, after the Chinese fashion, with all its tackle.

Two flagons of gold, embossed, of Japan, to stand on a cupboard, which may be transported upon occasion in a Japan[2] trunk, where their places are marked.

---

[1] Not all the French editions of Chaumont contain complete lists of presents, and the 1687 English translator gives up half-way, saying he was "weary of relating" them.

[2] 'Of Japan' and 'Japan work' may mean lacquerware (for which 'varnished' is also sometimes used in the original) or may indeed mean the objects come from Japan, which was most probably the case with the silverware. A fuller discussion of these presents is found in Michael Smithies, ed., *The Discourses of the First Siamese*

A javelin covered with embossed work after the Japan manner.

Two small golden cups, with their small bowls, on a fairly high stand, very well wrought Japan work.

Two small golden cups without covers, well-wrought embossed work of Japan.

A golden porringer, of finest Japan work.

Two Chinese ladies, each of them on a peacock, carrying in their hands a small silver cup, enamelled, the peacocks by turning a spring walk on a table, according to the way they are placed, the cups staying upright in their hands.

Two silver trunks, with best embossed Japan work, and one part in steel.

Two great silver flaggons, with two gilded lions, with two great basins all of the same finest Japan work.

Two great covered goblets of silver, with two big basins, all of finest Japan work.

A great open silver goblet with its silver basin.

An ewer and basin of silver, on four fronts of same, Japan work.

Two silver goblets, English fashion, to drink beer in, with two saucers, Japan work.

Two pairs of chocolate dishes with their silver covers, Japan work.

Two fairly large Japan cups.

Two other smaller cups, with their silver dishes, to drink liquors out of, both covered by a silver sprig, of the same work.

Two great silver water coolers, Chinese fashion, with their dishes, the same Japan work.

Ambassadors to France 1686-7 together with the List of their Presents to the Court (Bangkok, Siam Society, 1986).

Two Chinese horsemen carrying in their hands two small cups, who walk by a motion by springs, all of silver in the Chinese fashion.

Two ewers on two tortoises, all silver, and embossed, to contain water for washing one's hands, China work.

Two silver covers, Japan work, which had a motion by a spring, and carry each of them a small cup.

Two great Japan cabinets, flowerdeluced within, set forth with silver, and finely varnished, Japan work.

Two indifferently-sized trunks, set forth with silver, of the same work, but without fleurs-de-lis.

Two small tortoiseshell cabinets, set out with silver, much esteemed Japan work.

Four big salvers, set out with silver, Japan work.

A little silver cabinet, embellished with Japan work.

Two stands, varnished, set with silver, Japan work, one being of tortoiseshell.

A varnished table, adorned with silver, Japan work.

Two screens in Japan wood, containing six leaves, which is a present sent by the Emperor of Japan to the King of Siam.

Another silk screen on a blue background, showing many birds and flowers in relief, likewise of six panels, made at Siam.

Another screen larger than the two former ones, containing twelve leaves, which can be displayed by day and by night, Peking work.

Two great leaves of paper forming perspective views, in one of which are all sorts of China birds, in the other flowers.

A table service from the Emperor of Japan, very curiously and intricately worked.

A field service for a great Japan lord, well varnished.

Twenty-six kinds of salvers, of finest Japan varnish.

A small Japan cabinet which passes for a curiosity.

A small varnished table of Japan.

Two small coffers full of small varnished cups of Japan.

Two other small varnished trunks, scarlet outside and black within, Japan work.

A great round red varnished box, Japan work.

Two silk lanthorns with figures, very curious work from Tonkin.

Two other round lanthorns, the bigger of a single piece of horn, each with its silvered decoration.

Two morning gowns from Japan, of extraordinary beauty, one purple, the other scarlet.

A Persian carpet, with a gold background and many colours.

A carpet of red velvet edged with gold, and a green velvet border also edged with gold.

A Chinese carpet with a scarlet background and many flowers.

Two Hindustan carpets, one with a white silk background and gold flowers, and one of multicoloured silk.

Nine pieces of bezoar of several animals.

Two trunks of black lacquered wood with gold flowers, Japan work.

Two kinds of halberds, the iron being made in Siam, set with tambac, the wood being of Japan, in a gilded Japan wood scabbard.

Fifteen hundred or fifteen hundred and fifty pieces of porcelain, the best and most curious of all the Indies; more than two hundred and fifty being very fine, and comprising many cups, plates, small dishes, and big vases of all shapes and sizes.

Presents from the King of Siam to Monseigneur the Dauphin[3]

Two sabres of Japan, set out with tambac, which are two blades of large swords at the end of a long wooden staff.

An ewer and its golden basin, Japan work.

A golden teapot.

A small golden goblet decorated with a sprig, very curious Japan work.

A golden cup, Japan work.

A cup with a small silver plate, Japan work.

A silver chocolate pot, with golden flowers.

Another silver chocolate pot with golden flowers in high relief, Japan work.

Two silver covered pots.

Two silver escritoires, Japan work.

Two cups inlaid with silver, adorned with gold.

A great silver cup with gilded decoration, curious Japan work.

Two silver cups from Japan.

Two small cups with their small dishes of silver, with gilded decoration.

Two other small cups, surrounded by sprigs with their basins, the whole of silver.

Two other small cups of another fashion.

A small silver tobacco box, Japan work.

A great vase with a silver basin of Japan, very fine.

Two Japan ladies, who carry each of them in their hands a little dish, with a silver cup in it, and when the cup is full, the ladies walk about.

A silver crab bearing a cup upon its back and which walks about because of a spring.

---

[1]   The Dauphin was Louis XIV's son by his queen (Maria-Theresa of Austria, 1638-1683, daughter of Phillip IV of Spain), and was twenty-six years old in 1686; he died of smallpox four years before his father, in 1711.

A goblet made of a single stone with leaf decoration around, China work.

A cup covered with sprigs decorated with fruit and flowers.

A small cup of stone surrounded by a snake.

Two small stone cups, of admirable workmanship.

A China lion made from a single stone.

A small ewer made from a single stone.

Two Japan dressing gowns, well worked.

A green velvet carpet with flowers, from Hindustan.

A silk flowered carpet of divers colours.

A silk and velvet gold-coloured carpet from Hindustan.

A cloth flowered carpet, also of divers colours.

Two chased silver cabinets, Japan work.

A small trunk partly of red brass, partly lacquered, Japan work.

Two silver decorated stands, one of tortoiseshell, and one lacquered from Japan.

Four large salvers edged with silver.

A small silver-decorated chest.

Twenty-one large and small salvers, very fine, Japan work.

Two tortoiseshell salt cellars, and three others, lacquered, from Japan, one silver embellished.

A small lacquered table, Japan work.

A small flat tortoiseshell chest.

A small salt cellar, Japan work.

A covered drawer with partitions.

A small chest containing twelve others, lacquered Japan work.

A large box with its salver, black lacquered and with gold flowers.

Two small boxes of red lacquer.

A dinner set, for the house of a Japanese noble.

Two silk lanthorns of various kinds of flowers, embellished with silver.

A small cabinet, Japan work.

Two silk screens from Japan, of admirable workmanship.

Three chests, two one and one black, lacquered, from Japan.

Six and a half pounds of eaglewood.

In addition, eighty-four pieces of porcelain, both big and small, all very fine.

Presents sent by the Princess Queen of Siam to Madame la Dauphine [4]

A gold ewer, Japan work.

A round gold-covered box, of Japan.

A small gold chocolate pot, of Japan.

A small round box covered with gold, of Japan.

A small gold cup with a silver dish, Japan work.

A big silver flask mounted by a lion, Japan relief work, with a large silver basin.

Two other similar vases, only smaller.

Two silver chocolate pots, Japan relief work.

Two other silver chocolate pots, of Japan.

Two big silver cups, of Japan.

Two small cups with silver basins, of Japan.

Two other smaller cups with their silver basins entwined with flowers, of Japan.

A big silver heart, of Japan.

Two ladies of Japan, gilded and enamelled silver, each of which carries a small cup in her hands, and which move by springs.

[1] The Princess Queen of Siam was King Narai's only child, Krom Luang Yothathep; La Loubère (1693:52) notes she was also considered his wife after the death of his queen. The Dauphiness was Marie-Anne Christine of Bavaria, who died in 1690.

A small silver-handled box, of Japan.

A twelve panelled screen, of Japan wood, inlaid with birds and trees, with the edges gilded.

A bigger screen with twelve panels made of silk on a violet background, inlaid with animals and trees in many colours.

Another smaller silk screen, with very fine Chinese painting.

Two cabinets in white lacquered wood, with flowers of divers colours, and gilded brass ornaments.

Two Japanese dressing gowns, one of extraordinary beauty, the other more ordinary.

A tortoiseshell writing case with dividers.

Two lacquered bookstands edged with silver.

Twenty-one kinds of salvers, Japan work.

Four small lacquered double boxes, of Japan.

A flat box, and two others, of Japanese silk.

Two tortoiseshell writing cases, of Japan.

Two others, lacquered, of Japan.

A round red box, garnished with silver, of Japan.

Seven different small boxes, lacquered, of Japan.

A square box with twelve others, smaller, of Japan.

A Japanese lady's dressing set in tortoiseshell.

An eight-sided Japan chest full of very curious small boxes.

Another red lacquered Japanese lady's dressing set.

A tortoiseshell shelf adorned with silver.

A small red lacquered table, of Japan.

Another small lacquered table, of Japan.

A very fine lacquered cabinet.

Three other very fine varnished cabinets of Japan, adorned with gilded brass.

A big round double box with gold flowers.

A covered drawer with many dividers.

Two big salvers, adorned with silver.

Two other big lacquered salvers, of Japan.

Two red lacquered chests, adorned with silver.

Two lacquered boxes with gold and green flowers.

A bamboo and silk fan.

Two chests of black lacquer and gilded brass.

In addition, six hundred and forty pieces of very fine porcelain.

Presents from the Princess Queen of Siam to the Duke of Burgundy[1]

A small gold chocolate pot with its small silver tray, Japan work.

A silver vase, in which there are little men who appear when there is water inside.

A round box, covered with silver, Japan work.

A small covered silver vase, mounted by a lion, of Japan.

A small cup with two handles in its silver basin, Japan work.

Another small cup with its silver basin, Japan work in relief.

A Chinese lady of silver and amber which moves by springs.

Three small cabinets made in Macao, capital of Japan [!], bedecked with silver.

Four similar small boxes.

A lady's dressing set, of Japan.

A lacquered writing case, of Japan.

A small lacquered cabinet with two doors, adorned with gilded brass.

A lacquered bookrest of Japan, adorned with silver.

---

[1] The Duke of Burgundy was the eldest son of the Dauphin, and aged four in 1686; he died in 1712, and his son succeeded Louis XIV on his death in 1715.

A lacquered table of Japan.

A red box, work of China.

A small six-panelled screen from China.

A lacquered writing case of Japan, with gold flowers.

A porcelain dog.

In addition, thirty-two small pieces of porcelain.

A similar gift was made by the Princess Queen of Siam to the Duke of Anjou.[1]

Mr Constance's presents to the king

A great gold chain, finely wrought.

A goblet covered with silver, with relief work in gold.

Two small silver trunks, of Japan.

Three silver chocolate dishes, of Japan.

A great silver dish with six sides, of Japan.

Two four-sided dishes, with a handle of the same work.

Two dishes standing on three feet with two ears, of Japan.

Two other dishes of different kinds, but of the same work.

Two round dishes of the same work.

Two others, eight-sided, without feet, with ears.

A silver teapot also used for making ginseng.

Two smaller dishes with ears of the same work.

Two chocolate cups of the same work.

Four different small pieces to burn perfumes, after the China and Japan fashion.

A small tobacco box of the same work.

A box with its basin of tambac.

Porcelains:

---

[1] The Duke of Anjou was the second son of the Dauphin, aged three in 1686; he became Phillip V of Spain, reigning from 1700 to his death in 1746. He was mentioned, like his brother, earlier in the text.

Twelve fine ancient plates, blue-coloured.

Twelve others, very old, red and blue.

Twelve other plates of Japan, of different colours.

Six of another sort, eight-sided, of Japan.

An open-work dish, of Japan.

Six small dishes, with underplates, very old, of China.

Two larger dishes with their basins, of very fine workmanship.

Six small cups with their underplates, of old workmanship.

Two plates of very fine ancient China work.

Six varnished wood plates with enamelled brass.

Three extraordinary little teapots from China.

A bird of prey, of Japan.

Two ducks, of Japan.

Two white well-shaped dogs, of Japan.

A small earthenware China teapot which can also be used for making ginseng, according to one's wish.

Sixteen different sorts of earthenware of Pattani, with a with a Mingal lid [?], for boiling water.

Twenty-five stone figures from China.

Two six-sided screens, of Japan.

Two cabinets of the same work.

Two of another fashion, also of Japan.

A box to put combs in, of Japanese lacquer.

Four feet varnished for a bed, of Japan.

A lady's service, of Japan.

Two powder boxes, of Japan.

Two other boxes with tiny compartments, for making medicines.

Another lady's service, of Japan.

Another service, different.

Two boxes, three each in one, of Japan.

A small screen of eight sides, from China, which the king uses to put on a table.

A small salver, of Japan.

Another salver where there are three sections for putting three cups of tea thereon.

Two agate spoons.

A lady of Siam's mantle, gilded, of Pattani silk, to serve as a sample.

A piece of Kashmir stuff to serve as a sample, to see if it would be useful to the king, and His Majesty has only to issue the order.

Two extraordinary teapots full of such tea as the Emperor of China uses.

A smaller and still more wonderful teapot.

A measure of eight taels of ginseng, placed in the hands of the ambassador himself to take care of.

A Japan trunk full of birds' nests.

Seven great porcelain vases of different kinds, three from China and four from Japan.

Two chaplets of eaglewood, one set with gold and the other with tambac.

Three rhinoceros horns, one of which is from a buffalo.

Two birds of prey, of porcelain.

Mr Constance's presents to the Marquis de Seignelay[1]

A gold cup, Japan work.

Two silver salt cellars.

Two silver chocolate pots.

A bigger silver chocolate pot.

A big silver cup.

Two small covered vases, similar.

A small cup with its covered basin, similar.

Two small silver flasks, Japan work.

A table set of a Japanese noble, lacquered black with gold flowers.

[1]   Secretary of State for the Navy.

Eight different salvers of Japan.

A red eight-sided box with other smaller boxes inside.

A small lacquer chest, adorned with silver.

A small lacquer writing case.

A small portable chest with four levels.

A black lacquered box with three levels, with gold flowers.

A plain writing case, of Japan.

A covered lacquered drawer, of Japan.

A small tortoiseshell chest of Japan, very fine.

Four very curious small lacquered boxes.

A very fine Japanese dressing gown.

Two rhinoceros horns.

Two very curious screens worked in the Chinese manner, each with eighteen panels, lacquered.

A very curious large cabinet, of Japan.

A chest full of birds' nests.

Four boxes of tea.

In addition, one hundred and sixty large and small pieces of porcelain, all fine, and some very old.

There was a similar gift from Mr Constance to the Marquis de Croissy[1].

[Other persons receiving presents]

I make no mention here of the gifts to the ambassador nor to the Abbé de Choisy, which were most magnificent.

---

[1]   Secretary of State for Foreign Affairs.

A river scene on the Chao Phya, aboard a junk (such as is found in the bas-reliefs in the Bayon).

ABBÉ DE CHOISY
THREE TEXTS RELATING TO
THE EMBASSY TO SIAM 1685

A nobleman being transported by barge on the Chao Phya.

ABBÉ DE CHOISY

MEMORANDUM ON RELIGION IN SIAM[1]

On board the *Oiseau*, 1 January 1686

Although I have written until now, and am resolved to
continue, the *Journal* of my voyage, I thought it appropriate
to give a particular account which I shall divulge to no one,
in which I shall disclose all the details of the negotiations
which were conducted in Siam. There were many things
which need to remain secret. It is true that I am not the
ambassador [in charge], but I knew a part of what occurred,
and shall be pleased on my return to France to be able to
give an account of my conduct if I have the honour of being
asked for it.

When the Chevalier de Chaumont was named by the
king his ambassador to the King of Siam, he was charged
with everything, without any participation on my part. The
Marquis de Seignelay[2] merely informed me that His
Majesty had named me to stay close to the King of Siam in

---

[1] This originally untitled manuscript memorandum is preserved in the
archives of the Foreign Missions in Paris, covered with sea water
stains. It was partially published in French in 1920 by Launay, and in
toto by Dirk Van der Cruysse in his edition of Choisy's *Journal du
Voyage de Siam* (Paris, Fayard, 1995).

[2] Jean-Baptiste Colbert (1651-1690), Marquis de Seignelay, Secretary of
State for the Navy, was the son of Colbert and nephew of Croissy,
Secretary of State for Foreign Affairs.

the stead of the Chevalier de Chaumont if, after the farewell audience, some matters remained to be concluded, and that, if the said chevalier died en route, His Majesty named me to succeed him and conduct the embassy. I embarked with these words, having neither written orders from the king nor instructions, so that, seeing I was entirely at the discretion of the ambassador, I thought it necessary to obtain his good favour. I hardly knew him. I observed his character, and finding him very reserved, I did not throw myself at his head: a lot of civility towards His Excellency, often in my cabin where I studied, ever gay, ever happy. He said nothing to me of official matters, and I nothing to him, and we spent a full six months as if we had nothing to sort out together. I lived in the same fashion with the ship's officers, without entering into their quarrels, not even to settle them: there were plenty of people who took on the task without being asked. I was the friend of everyone, and confident of no one.

However, seeing I had almost arrived in Siam without the ambassador saying a word to me about what he was going to do there, I began to believe he would say nothing at all to me, and I had resolved to go and stay at the Seminary,[1] to take holy orders, and to stay until it was time to re-embark. I had this intention when the Bishop of Metellopolis[2] and the Abbé de Lionne[3] came on board; the

[1] In Mahapram, north of Ayutthaya. Choisy did in fact take orders, in Lopburi in December 1685. There is no mention here of the passage, given below, found in both the *History of the Church* Vol. XI and his *Memoirs...*, of the way Choisy succeeded, during the outward journey, of having Chaumont take him into his confidence concerning their mission in Siam.

[2] The Bishop of Metellopolis, Mgr Louis Laneau (1637-1696), in Siam from 1664; he became apostolic vicar in Siam from 1673 in charge of the French mission in Ayutthaya until his death.

[3] Abbé Artus de Lionne (1655-1713), son of a minister, a Missionary in the Far East since 1681. He left Siam in 1688 as Bishop of Rosalie for China.

bishop went into the ambassador's cabin and the Abbé into mine.

I told him first of all that the ambassador was going to propose to the King of Siam, on behalf of our king, that he became a Christian. He seemed surprised at this suggestion and told me frankly that things had not reached that point; that in truth the King of Siam favoured the Christian religion in everything; that he had churches built; that he gave money to the Missionaries; that he had helped the Bishop of Heliopolis[1] to enter China; but that, for changing religion, he did not believe he had even thought of it, and it would probably not be a trifling matter just to suggest it to him. I told him that our king, in sending an ambassador here, thought things were more advanced; that he had been told that the King of Siam was persuaded of the falsity of his own religion; that he no longer went to the temples of his gods; that he had already given up several superstitions, and that he only had to be pushed a little for him to embrace the true religion. He replied that the King of Siam did not appear over-attached to his idols, but that it was still a long way from that to receiving baptism.

With this, the ambassador came up on deck, the Abbé de Lionne went to greet him and told him in front of me that he was very surprised at what I had told him, and repeated in a few words the same conversation he had had with me. The bishop had in great secrecy said the same thing to the ambassador, so that our conversation became common in spite of ourselves, and this was the first time I spoke to the ambassador of matters concerning the embassy. He had shown until then all manner of civilities and concern, but ever about general news and topics.

---

[1]   Mgr François Pallu, apostolic vicar of Tonkin and five Chinese provinces; he left Siam in 1683 and died in China the following year.

The bishop showed himself very friendly towards me, and supposing he ought to have nothing hidden from me, he told me frankly the state of affairs. He had received letters from the gentlemen in the Paris Seminary, who advised him to place confidence in me. Thus was I involved. A council was held about the measures to be taken. Mr Vachet was not called as he had gone to Siam[1] to give news of our arrival. The bishop disclosed that the king left the conduct of his affairs to Mr Constance [Phaulkon] who, without wishing to have the titles, performed all the duties and had full authority; that this Mr Constance was very intelligent and one should not think of doing anything except through him; that he had, therefore, to be won over; that he was not troubled about money, but that in flattering him in matters where his honour was involved he was very sensitive, and could be made to bring about the impossible. This appeared very reasonable, and it was decided to follow this course of action.

The ambassador nevertheless proceeded to Siam with all imaginable pomp, and stayed a week at the Tabanque[2] a league away from the town to decide on the manner of his entry and audience. Mr Constance came to see him from the king and decided everything with him. The Abbé de Lionne was charged with presenting his compliments and assuring him that the ambassador wished to follow his advice in everything; that coming from the ends of the earth in the cause of [the Catholic] religion, he thought himself most fortunate to be able to deal with a Christian minister

---

[1] To Ayutthaya; Father Bénigne Vachet (1641-1720) was the French Missionary interpreter who had accompanied the two Siamese envoys to France in 1684 and who had sown the seed in the ears of the king's confessor, Father de La Chaize, that King Narai could be converted.

[2] The custom house; the word appears to be a Portuguese corruption, *tabanaca*, of the Malay term for custom house, *pabean*.

as clever and as well intentioned as he; and that, moreover, if things turned out as His Most Christian Majesty hoped, he could be assured of a solid reward. These compliments were very well received and he promised miracles. He even began to give advice to the ambassador, for example showing him how to call the principal mandarins who were charged with escorting him and to formulate to them the many difficulties concerning his audience, so that the king would charge one of his ministers to arrange these matters with His Excellency, foreseeing that this would fall to him, which happened as he had planned.

Until then, I was in no way involved. The meetings took place between the ambassador, the bishop and Mr Constance, and when he left, either the ambassador or the bishop, or both together, told me what had passed and what had been decided.

A great difficulty arose. Mr Constance wanted to have the king's letter carried in triumph on a barge by itself, with the ambassador in another, and desired that, when the landing place had been reached, it be carried again triumphantly throughout the town and the palace enclosures. The ambassador did not wish to relinquish his letter, and stuck firmly to European customs. We were all agreed that one had to accommodate oneself to the customs of the country in matters which, far from being shameful, were still more honorable, and that one could not demonstrate honours too great to the king's letter. With that, I suggested to the ambassador that instead of putting the letter into the hands of the Siamese mandarins, it should be given to me to carry it in view of everyone in a golden dish into the palace courtyards and to the audience. He agreed to this and Mr Constance likewise, who simply wanted the letter to be seen by the people. In this way I gave myself a very honorable place, I who was rather embarrassed in these matters, having a position no more than in form. A royal barge was given to me alone, I went to the audience at the side of the ambassador, I entered upright without objections and had my position decided next to the ambassador, so that in the end it was difficult for His Excellency to have any audience, public or private, without my being called [to attend].

There was another great obstacle over presenting the letter. Never had an ambassador presented a letter to the King of Siam; ordinarily it was placed in the hands of the Barcalon[1] the previous day, who had it translated into Siamese, and the day of the audience the Barcalon gave it to the king. The ambassador declared to Mr Constance that he wished to place it into His Majesty's own hands. He was obdurate. This had to be done. But a small incident arose which I have described at length in my *Journal*,[2] in which the ambassador surpassed himself and showed resolution and presence of mind.

After the entrance and the audience, the details of which are in my *Journal*, we began to discuss business. Mr Constance came to see the ambassador several times. He was sometimes three hours in conversation with the bishop, who served as interpreter, and on leaving he usually said to me "Everything is going well". In the end, one evening the bishop said to me that I would certainly stay on in Siam. I spoke about this in front of him to the ambassador, who did not seem too distant from the proposal, though he spoke less assuredly. A Missionary named Paumard,[3] with whom Mr Constance shares many confidences, told me the same

---

[1] Barcalon, the *Phra Klang*, minister of trade and consequently with jurisdiction over foreigners.

[2] The incident appears in Choisy's entry for 18 October 1685 and is described in Chaumont's Chapter 3.

[3] Etienne Paumard (1640-1690), sometimes Paumart, was a Missionary in Siam from 1676 with some medical knowledge which gained him favour with Phaulkon and the court.

day that Mr Constance had positively told him that he wished his neck would be broken if I did not stay in Siam.

With this, I was overcome with joy. I knew I could not stay in Siam as the king's minister unless the King of Siam wished to take instruction in the Christian religion, and I considered that, if wise people assured me I would stay, matters concerning religion must be in good standing. I only entertained these agreeable thoughts a few moments. I thought about all that the bishop and the Abbé de Lionne had told me on our arrival of the little likelihood there was of the conversion of the king. I remembered that Mr Constance had several times said that one had to proceed very gently in this matter, and it occurred to me that perhaps he was deceiving both the ambassador and the bishop. These are certainly two saints who spend four hours in prayer every evening, but they had not taken part in many negotiations and could be tricked by a canny minister.

However, this matter was sufficiently important to me to need to know the truth. This is what I did to obtain it. I requested the ambassador to give me a copy of that part of his orders where mention was made of me. I had not wished to speak of this before, thinking he would give it to me of his own accord. But on this occasion, seeing that he never mentioned it, and that as it was absolutely essential for me to make my arrangements, I boldly asked him and he could not refuse my request. He took his orders from his trunk and in front of me copied the sections concerning myself. I saw that the king did not wish me to remain in Siam except with the almost certain result of the conversion of the king, to assist in his baptism.

It then became necessary to see where we were with this almost certain conversion of the king. I spoke about this separately to the ambassador and the bishop. They told me that the King of Siam was dreadfully afraid of the Dutch and to have the protection of our king he would do anything; that perhaps he would not become a Christian out of conviction, but what did it matter, providing he did so and that his subjects followed his example; that on reading our king's letter he had said in front of all his mandarins: "Ah ha, the King of France wants me to share his religion; I am obliged to him and can see his friendship is truly disinterested"; that His Majesty did not appear to be in the least angered by this proposal; that he had added, "Ah well, one must not annoy the King of France, but I do not yet know what his religion is. I must obtain instruction, and if I see the truth, I am willing to follow it." They added that Mr Constance had protested he would willingly give his life to be able to bring about such an important matter, but it had to be conducted gently, and since the ambassador was obliged to return in December, it would be for me to arrange that; that the Most Christian King in his letter did not seek anything other than that, except that the king take instruction in the Christian religion, and he was ready to do this by giving private audiences with the bishop who could speak to him as long as he wished about religion.

This seemed rather rich. However, as I was beginning to know the ambassador and the bishop as good people who easily allowed themselves to be persuaded by what they wanted, I did not think I would be disposed of for that. I told them that the more the King of Siam was afraid of the Dutch, the more his fine words were suspect in my eyes, and perhaps would stretch out his instruction for ten years to have our king's protection in the meantime; that nevertheless I placed myself in the prudent hands of the ambassador; that I would be delighted to remain in Siam; that I had only come for this, and that, as soon as the ambassador gave the word, I would start to prepare my retinue. This is what I said, though resolved not to leave it at that.

I saw clearly that only Mr Constance could let me know the truth. I resolved to gain his friendship. I talked about him for several days with Mr Paumard. I told him I knew that Mr Constance was the protector of the [Catholic] religion in the Indies. I had him tell me the whole story of his life. I wrote memoranda about this.[1] I told him that when he wished, I would tell him all that I knew about the European courts, and I did this; that this was absolutely necessary for a minister. I praised his intelligence, his liberality, his zeal. In short, by means of Mr Paumard, who faithfully related to him all that I said, I persuaded him that I wanted to count among his friends. I even gave him some small pieces of advice on his conduct with the French party, on the different ways he should use with each. I advised him to induce some honest pride in the ambassadors he was sending to France, so that, on leaving Siam, they abandoned the submissive and enslaved look that even the greatest lords have here, which would not please in France where it was expected that people of quality were very civil and conscious of their dignity. He received all this admirably well, and I noticed that on leaving the ambassador, he always sought me out and showed me much consideration.

An amusing incident occurred. I went to see him, he received me well, but he had me sit in a very ambiguous position, and one could doubt if he had shaken hands with me. Moreover, throughout we spoke in Portuguese. I styled him as *Vossa Senhoria*,[2] and he styled me as *Vossa Mercê*,[3] which is very different. I left very annoyed. I sent for Mr Paumard and had him tell Mr Constance that I would style him as he treated me, and doubtless affairs of state had

---

[1]   No memoranda are known to exist.
[2]   Your Lordship.
[3]   Your Grace, but without the concept in English of addressing a duke or an archbishop; more like Your Reverence or 'My good sir'.

prevented him considering what he had just done. It is hard to believe how much this little sign of strength improved his opinion of me. He repeated a hundred times *Vossa Senhoria* on the next occasion, and overwhelmed me with honours and attention.

When I thought I had made some small progress in his graces, one evening, without speaking of it to anyone, I went to seek him out and first of all said to him in the French manner that I wished to speak with him at leisure. He had everyone leave. I then told him that I was going to give him a signal mark of confidence, that what I wished most in the world was to stay in Siam. And with that I told him all that I had done to come here as ambassador, and that I hoped he would assist in letting me stay. He interrupted me to say that I would for certain remain; that the King of France in his letter asked only that the King of Siam take instruction, and he was ready to be so instructed. "But," I said, "for me to stay here, the ambassador must have definite confirmation, and the King of Siam needs write firmly in these terms." "All that," he replied, "will be done." "Very well then," I said, "I am content. I needed nothing more for me to stay here, and here are the king's orders on the subject." I showed him a part of the orders I had extracted from the ambassador. This mark of confidence gave him great pleasure. Confidences then followed from his side.

We changed the subject, and after speaking for two hours as if it were necessary for me to stay in Siam, I said to him, laughing, "Frankly, I find it hard to believe the King of Siam wants to become a Christian. There are nothing but talapoins[1] here. There is not a single Christian mandarin and if he asked my personal opinion, I do not know what I would advise him. But you must not tell the ambassador

---

[1]   Buddhist monks.

that, for he would not leave me here!" He replied in the same tone, "You are right; so he will not become a Christian, and even for the good of the [Catholic] religion, it would not be politic for him to convert too quickly. One has to start by converting a part of the kingdom. Has one ever seen a king change his religion without having [it established in] a large part in his realm? Moreover the king is old and in ill-health. Everything will change on his death, and perhaps the Christian religion will be persecuted as being the cause of disorder."

I thanked him profusely for his honesty. He carried on and told me that at the first audience he had not dared tell the king everything the ambassador had said about religion because of the mandarins who were present, and until reading the letter from the King of France, His Majesty had not known that all this great embassy had but the aim of his conversion; that His Majesty had opened his heart to him on this subject; that he was persuaded that all religions were good; that he had even said, "You are Christian; if you adopted my religion, I would think you a knave"; that he did not cease to be very obliged to the King of France; that he only acted out of friendship and that he must not be displeased, and that on this point he had assured the ambassador that all would go well; that on his return to France the king would be very pleased with his negotiations; that he would bear letters giving great hope of the conversion of the King of Siam; that finally God was the master of all things and one did not know what could happen.

I let him say anything he wanted; it was a torrent of truth which I was careful not to stop. When he had finished, I began again to praise his good intentions and let him understand that what would please our king the most would be equal sincerity; that one had to think of the solid foundation of religion and to take just measures; that since there was little likelihood of the conversion of the king, one had to think of the conversion of the kingdom, obtain privileges for the [Catholic] religion to try and convert the mandarins and to let the grace of God work on the king's person, who through his moral virtues seemed to deserve it. He said I was right, and that had always been his opinion; that he would not wish to press the king on the subject of religion, but the ambassador had absolutely insisted upon it. With that I took my time and said to him, "If you wish, we shall have the ambassador take other dispositions. I have only to tell him something of what you have told me. He is a sensible person he will see that there is no alternative to adopting and following your opinion." He replied that he wished it so, in the hope that he had of doing by the ambassador all that he desired, and I was very pleased to have obtained from him permission to disclose the truth to the ambassador who had so much interest in knowing this.

We separated after four hours of conversation very pleased with one another, and I returned to our lodging to give thanks to God for having revealed the truth to me. I saw clearly from that moment that I would not stay on in Siam, and afterwards thought a hundred times of the idiotic figure I would have cut. The ambassador would have returned to France, proud and triumphant, and said to the king, "Sire, I have left the Abbé de Choisy in Siam to take part in the baptism of the king." The bishop would have reported the same thing, and me too. The first news of such an important event would have been awaited impatiently. Two years, four years, six years would have passed by without any progress. Would there not be real cause to believe that by my poor conduct [of affairs] I had spoilt what the Chevalier de Chaumont had so well started?

The following day I related to the ambassador and the bishop all our conversation. They made me repeat it twice and had great difficulty in believing me. I offered to have

Mr Constance tell them the same thing himself, provided that they first thought fit to praise his sincerity. And indeed that very day he came to the ambassador's residence to confirm all that I had said.

As soon as he had gone, we resolved first that I would not stay on in Siam. The ambassador confessed that, on the strength of the likelihood of the king's conversion, he had resolved with the bishop to leave me there, but they had not yet wanted to tell me, nor to inform the Abbé de Lionne. It was decided then to try to obtain privileges for the new Christians and to gain advantages for the French [Indies] Company.

Mr Constance thought he had won the day, and that the ambassador, seeing the impossibility of converting the king, would abandon the enterprise and think of something else. But on the contrary we advised him to push his point, and indeed he presented the king with a very strong memorandum on [the Catholic] religion. Mr Constance then saw that he had shown his intentions too clearly, and protested several times that this memorandum would have the worst possible effect, and perhaps the king would make some disagreeable reply. We did not fear this, since His Majesty had said that the King of France should not be displeased, and on the contrary we considered the reply he was likely to give as a kind of engagement.

This reply was a month in coming. Mr Constance in the meanwhile amused the ambassador with tiger fights, promenades, and hunts. And I was occupied in choosing from the king's stores the finest that he had for the presents he wished to send to France. I said sometimes, and the Abbé de Lionne said the same, "But we must think of our business. The time to leave will soon arrive and nothing will be decided." We were told, "All will be done." We drafted nonetheless the articles for the privileges to be sought for the Christian religion, and Mr Véret, chief of the

French Company,[1] was ordered to draw up his requests. The ambassador spoke about this to the king in a private audience. His Majesty replied that he agreed to everything, and referred the execution of the matter to Mr Constance; he sought more time to prepare a proper written document.

Finally one evening Mr Constance came in search of the ambassador and said to him that the king wished to grant him an audience the following morning, and that he came to agree with him on what he would to say to His Majesty so that everyone would be satisfied. The bishop, the Abbé de Lionne and I were present at the conversation. Mr Vachet, who is more capable in these matters than any of us, was not there, because he had not been there from the beginning and it was not felt desirable to increase the number of advisors.

Mr Constance began by saying that the friendship which the King of Siam had for the French was completely disinterested; that he feared nothing for his policies; that, nevertheless, if the ambassador wished to please him, he would have the news announced that he had signed an offensive and defensive pact between the King of France and the kingdom of Siam; that this might be capable of restraining the Dutch in their designs; and that if he wished to do so, he would say this the next day to His Majesty at the audience. Mr Constance spoke in Portuguese, and the bishop and I explained what he said.

The ambassador replied immediately, without hesitation, that he would do this, and that he would announce everywhere that there was an offensive and defensive pact signed between the two kings. I was surprised he moved so quickly, and could not restrain myself from saying to him

[1]   Véret was the French factor, a Parisian jeweller who put personal profit before his Company's, who had come to Siam in 1685 with the French embassy.

in French in a low voice, "In truth, sir, you are promising much, and this is sufficiently important for us to think about it a little." He said nothing, showed by his vexed look that he was not pleased that I had taken the liberty to give him advice, and said again, more emphatically, "Yes, sir, I shall tell the king tomorrow that I am going to publish abroad that there is an offensive and defensive pact between His Majesty and the king my master, and I shall even mention it in passing to the governor-general in Batavia, and if I do not pass by there, I shall write to him about it." I said nothing more. The bishop and the Abbé de Lionne uttered not a sound, but it could be seen on their faces they they did not approve such precipitation.

Mr Constance, who understands French and had heard me perfectly, loudly thanked His Excellency, and complained bitterly that he had found everyone against him, myself included, and only the ambassador agreeable. He asked him again if he wished to leave behind some French officers. His Excellency was in a mood to agree to everything, and again said yes.

The following day we went to the audience. The ambassador kept his word and said still more to the king, going as far as offering to speak of this supposed pact to the head of the Dutch [East Indies] Company in Siam.[1] His Majesty said that this would be suspect and would appear untrue. On leaving the audience I praised the ambassador greatly for all that he had said. The damage was done; there was no remedy and I did not want to break with him. He was already beginning to act rather coldly towards me. I mended everything with ease and wiped out the audacity I had displayed the day before.

---

[1]   The Dutch Opperhoofd from 1685 to 1688 was Johannes Keijts, who related everything concerning the French embassy to his masters in Batavia.

That evening Mr Paumard came to find me on behalf of Mr Constance, and said that he would never have thought I would have been against him in the negotiation, that it did not depend on me whether the ambassador would refuse all that he had asked, and that after having promised him my friendship, as I had done, I should use it ill. I replied that when the service of God and my king obliged me to act, I could have no consideration for special friendships; that if the ambassador had listened to me he would not have agreed so readily; and that, at least before doing so, he ought to have tried to have the King of Siam speak about religion, and obtained in writing all the great privileges which were promised him, and would have concluded an advantageous treaty for the French Company; that I thought I was doing my duty, and I would do so again on a similar occasion, but that would not prevent me from rendering him a service when I was able, and that furthermore he was too much of an honest person not to think better of me. He said to Mr Paumard that that was just, but all the same from that time on he had no more confidence in me.

The King of Siam proposed himself in an audience that I should take presents to the Pope[1]. He [Phaulkon] prevented this on the pretext he did not have sufficiently beautiful presents. And when he brought the ambassador the privileges on religion and the treaty concerning the Company, I was not called, and in that he was not wrong, for assuredly I would not have let them pass as they are. The king agreed to everything, and Mr Constance included in every article conditions which reduced their value. The ambassador had only to insist and refuse all the conditions:

---

[1]   Innocent XI, Bernedotto Odescalchi (1611-89), elected pope in 1676, whom Choisy had met on his election.

Mr Constance would never have dared send that back to the king.

But what did he do? He always put off presenting written documents, saying they had to be copied, and that on leaving he would give everything in due form. The ambassador believed him, and in the farewell audience said positively to the King of Siam that he was content on all counts; that he thanked him for the great privileges he had granted the Christian religion and for everything he did in favour of the French Company. What is droll about this is that he had nothing in his hands, and had nothing in writing except when in the roads, ready to set sail, at a time when the means to discuss points no longer existed, and he had to accept what he was offered. It is not that I was against the view that the ambassador should agree on all the trifling matters with the King of Siam that he could without engaging our king, but I wanted him to command more respect, and that if the minister refused him something, he should address the king directly; he would have agreed to everything, for it is certain that this good king believed he had done everything possible of him.

He received the ambassador with extraordinary distinction. He is sending to France ambassadors and magnificent presents. We ask of him privileges for religion and the Company; he agrees to everything. The ambassador tells him he is happy. How could he not believe it? Is it his fault?

But perhaps I shall be asked, "Why did Mr Constance, a Christian, and a good one, not wish that the king be pressed on the subject of religion? Was he afraid he would concede too much?" Perhaps. He is a minister from overseas, hated by all the mandarins. If the king had converted and the people were against it, would they not have accused the Christian minister? Would they not have attacked him? And does one know if his zeal went as far as martyrdom? Moreover he perhaps followed his own thoughts and believed that the time was not yet ripe, even for the good of Christianity, for the king to become a Christian. As for business, it is natural that a minister trims as much as he can the privileges the king grants foreigners. He shows his merit in that, and puts his master in a position of obliging a second time by granting everything which had only been verbally agreed.

And to show that I was very far from preventing the ambassador from giving trifling pleasures to the King of Siam, it was I who advised him to give him an engineer to fortify his strong places.[1] He rejected the proposal I made at first, and then gave in when I protested that in his position I would do this, even if I had to pay the emoluments of the engineer. He realized that this would be a noble gesture, would greatly please the King of Siam, and would not displease our king. And in that, thank God, I had the interests of religion at heart, because if the fortified places of the King of Siam are in good condition and the Dutch dare not attack them, the missions are safe.

This is more or less what took place of greatest importance in the negotiations in Siam. Perhaps it was not impossible to extract more than we did, and never will a conjunction be more favourable to require the king to agree to almost all that was desired of him.[2]

---

[1] This was Sieur de La Mare, sometimes Lamarre, who stayed on in Siam; so did the Chevalier de Forbin, Chaumont's aide-de-camp, but at this juncture Choisy does not mention him (he is shown to have stayed on in Choisy's *Journal* entry for 10 December 1685).

[2] Choisy appears to have become aware of Phaulkon's manoeuvres only at the very end of his stay in Siam.

ABBÉ DE CHOISY

MEMORANDUM ON COMMERCE IN THE EAST INDIES

1686[1]

As I had several conversations with Mr Constance [Phaulkon] on the means of securely establishing the French [East Indies] Company in the Indies, and he is persuaded that this cannot be done without ruining the Dutch company, I am going to write down all that I managed to obtain from him on the subject. The Bishop of Metellopolis[2] and some junior servants of the Company have also told me some important things on this subject.

There is at present no question of declaring war on the Dutch, but it seems that it would be good politics to prepare to ruin them in the Indies when one wished to, which our king can easily do and at almost no cost. Firstly, the idea that they are so powerful in the Indies must be removed. It is true they have a great number of vessels and they maintain garrisons in more than fifty places,[3] but this

---

[1] This memorandum was written shortly after the one on religion, on board the *Oiseau* on Choisy's return journey from Siam to Brest. It is strongly anti-Dutch and in favour of the establishment of a French trading house in Songkhla. The memorandum in the Achives Nationales was published for the first time by Van der Cruysse in 1995 in his edition of Choisy's *Journal du voyage de Siam*.

[2] Mgr Louis Laneau.

[3] Choisy in his *Journal* entry for 26 August 1685 details the Dutch

is precisely where their weakness lies. All their forces are scattered in so many distant places that they could easily be beaten one after the other.

They have only 12,000 regular troops in all the Indies, and perhaps 100,000 natives who take up arms for them. Of these 12,000 men, few are Dutch; most are French, Flemings or Germans whom they treat very harshly, and all are revolted by their service and ready to desert on the first occasion. The Dutch only constitute a good number of the officers. They all shook in their shoes when Mr de La Haye[1] came to the Indies, and if he had orders to wage war on them, he would virtually have taken everyone he attacked. They had already sent to the Moluccas[2] all the French who were in Batavia.

Moreover their fortifications are suitable for defence against the natives, but they would hardly stand up against the disciples of Mr Vauban.[3] The famous fortress of Batavia is very ordinary, built on piles, and shakes each time a cannon is fired. Their forts in the Moluccas are nothing much.

Add to this that all the kings in the Indies are afraid of them and seek but to attack them. They are considered everywhere as usurpers. They have several kings in their prisons, and the most recent violence they have conducted

outposts in the Indies, after having obtained information about them during his brief stay in Batavia.

[1]   Jacob Blanquet de La Haye in 1670 led a fleet of eight ships to seize Trincomalee in Ceylon; the fleet was routed by the Dutch, all the French ships were sunk or taken, and the Dutch had to lend the French two vessels for the return to France of the 530 men who were still alive (out of 2,100 to start with). Choisy could hardly have chosen a more disastrous and unlikely example of French forces causing the Dutch to quake in the shoes.

[2]   The so-called spice islands in the east of the Indonesian archipelago.

[3]   Sébastien Le Prestre, Maréchal de Vauban, the military architect to Louis XIV.

against the King of Bantam[1] succeeded in turning all the Oriental monarchs against them. They thought they would be chased out of Tonkin but bought their way to remain. The King of Siam is not pleased with them. The kings of Cambodia, Johor, Jambi, Kedah and Pattani,[2] tributaries of Siam, would furnish at the first order a large number of war galleys. The Queen of Aceh[3] has proposed a pact against them to the King of Siam. The kings of the Moluccas groan under their tyranny. If so many monarchs, who are far from lacking courage, were maintained and led by the French, they would be capable of much.

Furthermore, although the Dutch Company obtains huge profits from trade, much must be deducted by the thieving of its junior officials. It is said that at the Siamese trading house[4] the officials steal regularly thirty per cent. One should also mention that their greatest profit arises from the Molucca islands which produce cloves and nutmegs. For the island of Ceylon, their expenses exceed their revenues because of the huge garrisons they have to maintain against the King of Kandy who continually wages war against them, apart from the fact that cinnamon which is extracted thence is not so dear as formerly.

They do everything they can to make themselves masters of all the pepper from the Malabar coast, and with impunity confiscate native boats loaded with it. They have

[1] Sultan Abdulfatah Ageng (Sultan Tirtayasa), r. 1651-1680, when he resigned in favour of his son, Sultan Haji, whose misbehaviour caused Ageng to attempt to seize the throne again. Haji called for Dutch help in 1682; Ageng was captured and imprisoned in 1683 in Batavia until his death.

[2] Kedah and Johor, Malay states on the peninsula, and Jambi in east Sumatra all sent tribute to Siam, though that from Jambi in particular was much more a commercial transaction than an indication of submission.

[3] Queen Anayet Syah Zagiryat ad-Din, r. 1677-1688.

[4] The Dutch 'factory' (trading post) at Ayutthaya.

virtually achieved their objective in taking Bantam and have nothing to fear, except if the French set up in the kingdom of Siam, and trade in pepper which has begun to be planted in the last few years, for if they had this as well, they could fix the price of pepper as high as they wished, as they have done for other spices, which makes them incomparably more powerful, because one can do without cloves and cinnamon, but not without pepper, which is equally necessary to everyone the world over. Indeed, since they took Bantam, pepper is said to have become much dearer in Surat and throughout the Indies.

As I have already said, the rest of all their commerce is nothing in comparison to this. They do not make as much profit in Japan as they did formerly. The officials of the King of Japan place a tax on all the goods they bring and require them to sell them at a fixed price or to take them back, nothing being allowed to be sold to individual merchants. Throughout the rest of the Indies, they are not better treated than the French or the English.

They lose a lot in their trade with Persia. They concluded a few years back a treaty with the King of Persia by which they undertook to take 600 bales of silk annually at a certain price. Recently silk of equal quality but much cheaper than that from Persia is now produced in Bengal, and the English have taken a large amount to Europe and sold it more cheaply than the Dutch. This makes them wish to renounce their treaty with the King of Persia, who will not hear speak of it. They set sail to try and make him submit by force and eighteen months ago sent six warships to Ormuz or Bandar Abbas to attack the Persians, and return then to Surat to require the government of the Great Mogul[1] to judge in their favour against several chiefs they were in conflict with. It is even said that they expected to

---

[1]   Aurangzeb, r. 1658-1707.

come to Bengal in the certitude they have that everything would give way before them.

As soon as their vessels arrived in Bandar Abbas, they sent envoys to the King of Persia to require him to abrogate the treaty concerning silk, to put to death or have his chief minister Atamaldoler placed in their hands, to exempt them from customs dues in Bandar Abbas, to be compensated for their losses over the silk treaty, and to be paid for the expense of arming their six warships. The King of Persia replied to these proposals by having all the Dutchmen in his states arrested and confiscating all the effects in three of their trading posts. They cruised some time before Bandar Abbas and in order not to retrace their steps withdrew to a deserted island, where the excessive heat caused the death of half their crews. The head of their trading post in Surat thinking these warships should return, had discretely withdrawn to Sualis,[1] but not seeing them come back, considered it prudent to return to Surat, and the government levied a heavy fine on him.

It can be seen from all these details that the Dutch draw their greatest profit from the Moluccas. And as they have placed a tax on cloves and nutmegs, when they have what they want, they burn what remains, which could easily fill several vessels, and they even give fifteen or twenty thousand *écus* every year to different princelings to burn all the nutmeg and clove trees in their lands. If they lost the Moluccas, or if the French or the English were well established in one of these islands, it is certain that the [Dutch] Company would collapse and in consequence the United Provinces to which the Company supplies money would lose half of its might.

As I have already said, it would not be very difficult to chase them off one such. They have only four or five rather

---

[1]   The small outer port of Surat.

poor fortresses. All the neighbouring rulers do but wait to throw off their yoke. Even the people are weary of their domination. They require them to buy their clothes and their victuals from the Company at the price they determine, and they are required to cultivate nutmeg and clove trees without being able to sell to anyone, even after having supplied the Company.

I think that one can conclude from all that I have said that it is not impossible to ruin, or at least seriously to disturb Dutch trade in the Indies. Here is a favourable occasion. The King of Siam is offering our king Singor,[1] which is easy to make a centre which would soon have considerable trade. It is nine degrees latitude north. Its situation is advantageous and naturally fortified. One could build a splendid port there at little expense. Medium-sized vessels could enter it and be in safety in all weathers. The road is only exposed to the north-east, but one could withdraw to Ligor[2] which is twenty leagues from Singor and where the port is extremely safe.[3]

Everything which passes through the Sunda and Malacca straits more or less passes in sight of Singor, so that with two or three vessels one could share a large part of the trade with China, the Manila lands, Borneo, etc. It would be possible, if war broke out, in the time that vessels come from China, to send some ships to the desert islands

---

[1]   Songkhla, sometimes Singora, in the south of Siam, between Nakhon Si Thammarat (Ligor) and Pattani. Others, including Vachet, had indicated this proposal; it was however something of a poisoned gift, since Songkhla was in almost continual revolt against Siamese rule, as can be seen from Choisy's own text below.

[2]   Nakhon Si Thammarat is at 8 degrees 30 minutes latitude north (Songkhla is in fact at a little more than 7 degrees, not 9); the port, in spite of Choisy's comments, is indifferent.

[3]   Choisy was no authority on the subject, and had neither been to Songkhla nor to Nakhon Si Thammarat.

of Pulocambi[1] which lie towards Cambodia to observe them as they pass, and even though these islands are uninhabited, water, wood, and fish are found there.

It is even said, and it is a gentleman who informed the Bishop of Metellopolis, that, having landed fortuitously on these islands, some Malays took him to a wood where he gathered a quantity of nutmegs which he sold very well in Macao. What casts somes doubt on this is that the Dutch know nothing of it, for if they did, they would seize these islands. But one could reply to that that they have not dared to do so up to now because some Cochin-Chinese had taken them and abandoned them but recently, and the Dutch want to have nothing to do with this nation which has treated them so ill;[2] apart from the fact that the nutmegs, being of small quantity, are not worth a great deal of trouble. As for planting them in other places, the people in the Indies are not sufficiently provident to think that far ahead.

Mr Vachet[3] has also told me that there is much cinnamon in Cochin-China, of good quality and very cheap. The Cochin-Chinese export it to China. There is also along the coasts of Siam, especially in places where eaglewood[4] is gathered, a type of cinnamon in truth coarser than that from Ceylon, but which has something of the smell of the clove and the nutmeg. The natives and even the Portuguese

---

[1] Pulau Cambi, but which islands Choisy has in mind is not clear; possibly Pulo Condor, the Con Son islands, off the southern tip of what is now Vietnam.

[2] The Dutch supported Tonkin in its struggle with Cochin-China.

[3] The Missionary Vachet was in Cochin-China from 1673 to 1680.

[4] Eaglewood, also known as agala wood, agalloch, calambac, aguilawood, and aloes wood: the fragrant resinous heartwood of the *aquilaria* which was much traded in the seventeenth century, and, according to Schouten (1636), was one of the more important trade items of Siam.

use it in their medicines instead of Singalese cinnamon which is very expensive. This costs almost nothing and one has but to cut it. A considerable trade could be conducted in this from Singor, as demonstrated in the attached memorandum.[1]

Moreover, if the French were established in Singor, they could take on pepper from the Malay coasts, but would have to watch out for the Dutch. A vessel from Macao went last year to Jambi which the Malays pillaged and would have killed all the Portuguese aboard if the Dutch had not saved their lives, either through compassion, or to give out that they had no hand in this matter.

It should also be pointed out that the King of Siam has promised to give the French Company a port in the Kingdom of Kedah which is tributary to him, on the same side as Junk Ceylon,[2] and in this way those in Singor could trade overland by river with those in Kedah without passing through the straits of Sunda or Malacca.

Moreover the French Company having by treaty all the pepper in the kingdom of Siam,[3] much of which is in Ligor, would not have to go far to collect it and would not be obliged to go to the expense of [establishing] a trading house.

I have forgotten to mention that the Dutch do not allow, under pain of death, the export from the Moluccas of any nutmeg or clove which could be planted elsewhere, and all that they sell are treated in such a manner that they cannot be planted.[4]

---

[1] No attached memorandum has survived.
[2] Phuket, on the Andaman Sea, a Siamese possession.
[3] The treaty of 1680 signed by André Deslandes on behalf of the French Indies Company; in fact Siam was not a major pepper producer.
[4] They were lightly grilled so they would not germinate.

Finally it is impossible to establish or to maintain the Christian religion in the Orient as long as the Dutch are the most powerful there. They are its greatest enemies and have expelled it from Japan, the Moluccas, Malacca, Ceylon, Cochin[1] and generally from all the places where they are the strongest.[2]

It is appropriate to say two words here of the history of Singor. In 1642 a Malay became master of Singor and revolted against the King of Siam. He fortified the site and soon attracted considerable trade there. The Siamese attacked him without success several times. He assumed after a time the title of King of Singor which he held until his death. His son succeeded him, but six years ago he was attacked in strength by the King of Siam who sent ships and a number of galleys there. He defended himself so well that he was only taken through the treason of the governor of a fort overlooking the town. The Siamese won over the governor and, having entered the fort, rained down flares over the town which burnt down the king's palace. They went on the assault during the consequent disorder and seized the site with their swords in their hand. They totally laid waste to the place for fear of another revolt starting there. This is the site which the King of Siam is offering our king with considerable territory.The English have loudly asked for it, and it would seem they are likely to get it if the French do not want it. The King of Siam is above all afraid that the Dutch will set up there in spite of him.[3]

---

[1] Kuchi Bandar, a town on the Indian coast of Malabar.

[2] Choisy exaggerates; the Dutch, though mostly Protestant, were generally neutral in religious matters. They became, though, markedly hostile to French Catholicism after the revocation of the Edict of Nantes in 1685.

[3] Choisy does not mention that both kings Prasat Thong and Narai had sought the assistance of the Dutch in putting down the frequent revolts in the south.

It is certain that if the French Company wants to be solidly established in the Indies, it must have a safe base. The Dutch have five. The Portuguese still have Macao. The English have Madras and Bombay. Even the Danes have Tranquebar on the Coromandel coast, and there is no situation more advantageous than that of Singor for trading with China, Japan, Tonkin, and Siam.

It should not be said that the Siamese trading post could undertake all this trade. One can see what happens when there is only one trading post by what happened to the English at Bantam. They were the masters in the councils of the King of Bantam. They commanded the best bastion in the town. It was the richest trading house they had in the Indies. Although they only traded with Siam, Tonkin and a few Chinese islands, they were all the same expelled in a shameful fashion. If they had had some other well fortified post, which the King of Bantam had several times offered them, the Dutch would never have dared undertake removing them.

Furthermore, to speak the truth, the Company will never have good trade in Siam as long as it does not have a completely free hand. It has been granted it. The King of Siam could refuse the ambassador nothing, but Mr Constance introduced certain conditions which made it useless. Here is the truth. Ten years ago all nations were free to trade in Siam. Only kaolin was granted in exclusivity to the Dutch[1] and some contraband goods like calambac,[2] aguila wood, birds' nests, etc. But since the death of the Barcalon, the brother of the first Siamese ambassador,[3] Mr Constance, to curry favour, has persuaded the king to

[1]   Choisy omits deer skins, which were sent to Japan in quantity.
[2]   Eaglewood; "aguila wood" which follows is the same thing.
[3]   The Phra Klang Kosathibodi or Kosa Lek, brother of Kosa Pan, who died, disgraced, in July 1683, with his effects seized.

undertake all trade, so that when the merchants come to Siam, the king takes all their goods in bulk and cheaply, and sells them retail very expensively. This has greatly increased his revenues, but in the long run it will ruin his trade. The foreign merchants are beginning to get discouraged and there are far fewer vessels [coming to Siam] than there used to be.[1] The king or the Company must set up a considerable establishment in Singor to attract commerce.

It will be said that the French are unhappy in the Indies. It is easy to see where that view comes from, the mistakes that have been made, and to establish the truth.

Madagascar was a good settlement. Mr de Chamargoux, a gentleman from Brittany, ruled all the island with a handful of people, but Mr de Montdevergue ruined everything. He abused his power. There was a regular council. He cared not two figs for it, armed the natives, often took their part against the French, and thought of his own enrichment.[2]

Mr de La Haye,[3] who followed him, did worse. He was a good land officer and a brave man, but wanted to be a sailor. He cashiered all the good naval officers because they

[1] Choisy, like Chaumont, puts his finger on the cause for the decline of Siam as a trading power from the end of the seventeeth century: royal absolutism and greed.

[2] Chamargoux only settled the south-east corner of the island; Montdevergue left in 1666 to colonize the island. The attempt was a fiasco, and Montdevergue was recalled, dying in prison while waiting trial. But French aims were as ever confused; the desire for converts as well as commerce was difficult to reconcile.

[3] This reference to La Haye is much less flattering than the earlier one, and more appropriate. La Haye was ordered to leave Montdevergue in Madagascar and improve the lot of the French settlers. He noted, on his way back to France in 1674, that those settlers who had not been butchered by their Madagascan servants had fled to Bourbon island (Réunion).

knew more than he did, and gave the command of his ships to ignorant men who caused them to be lost. He took with him the best troops from Madagascar, leaving inexperienced people who, after Mr de Chamargoux's death, harried at the wrong moment the people of Madagascar and could not hold out against them. He set up base in Trincomalee in Ceylon where the port is excellent. He concluded an advantageous treaty with the King of Kandy who did not ask for more than to have the French to support him against the Dutch. But instead of building a solid fortress, he was satisfied with building a small earthwork and to leave it in the hands of forty men the Dutch soon removed. It is not surprising that an enterprise miscarries when it is so badly conducted. There is nothing better than the defence of São Tomé. Actions worthy of Amadis[1] were carried out there. Mr de La Haye, with a hundred men, went five or six leagues in open country in full view of 40,000 horsemen, but had to give in for want of victuals, and six months earlier he could have had for 30,000 *écus* all the victuals he needed, for he was not short of money.[2]

To see what has to be done in establishing a post in the Indies, one should look at what the Dutch do. They are the masters there. They have ruined the Portuguese and the English, and looking at the situation of their affairs, it can be concluded that their procedure is not bad. Their fortresses are well supplied, their cities handsome, military discipline is well observed, the hospitals good, the temples

---

[1] *Amadis of Gaul* was a Spanish chivalric novel published by Ordóñez de Montalvo in 1508; its hero was a wandering knight and faithful lover.

[2] The French were besieged by the Dutch in São Tomé and the forces of the ruler of Golconda, and capitulated in 1674. They refused to buy São Tomé, so the rajah joined forces with the Dutch.

beautiful, externally religion is well-satisfied, justice is exact, there is magnificence in the senior people (the court of the Governor-General of Batavia is ostentatious), there is no familiarity with the natives. A councillor in Batavia considers himself a greater lord than the King of Makassar. But so much authority is not invested in a single head, for fear of it being abused; the Governor-General has only two votes in the Council. One rises in the ranks through merit, and one does not grow old in the Company's service without being promoted. An upstart from Europe is never given an important position in the Indies.

. One should base oneself on this for the establishment in Singor. A warlike governor of quality is needed, one who is businesslike, who does not have complete authority and who does not do with the council what he wills. Mr Caron[1] was chief of the French trading post in Surat, and in order not to be opposed, he divided the council, sending Mr Gouton to Masulipatam[2] and Messers Froter and Label to Persia. The council must be able, in case of death, to nominate officials who will be confirmed by the Company; letters should only be opened in full council, the Company's employees should be promoted step by step; the governor should depend on the Company and be on its payroll. A governor sent by the king never takes the merchants into sufficient consideration. Messers de Montdevergue and de La Haye failed on that score.

A general plan of the town must first be made. Companies should never die: look at Goa and Batavia. Complete

---

[1] François Caron (1600-1673) served in the VOC, the Dutch East Indies Company, in Asia for many years; on his retirement he agreed to join the French Indies Company, and founded its trading post in Surat.

[2] Also Masulipatnam and Machilipatnam, now Bandar, on the south-east Coromandel coast of India.

liberty in trade matters must first of all be given to all the merchants who come to Singor, of whatever nation and religion they be. The Dutch have done thus in Batavia, the English in Madras and Bombay. Soon Chinese will come there, because they are very badly treated in Siam, Batavia and throughout the Indies, and they will soon know that they are always well treated in a new post. The Mohammedans, who are called Moors in the Indies, will do likewise.

They will first of all seek to build temples and mosques. The Spanish and the Portuguese consistently refused this; the French will do no less in Singor, but that will not stop them from coming if they find it worth their while. Their foremost concern is profit. All the other nations in the Indies, Siamese, Peguans, Malays, Javanese, Cambodians, Chams,[1] Cochin-Chinese, Tonkinese, will come crowding in and will be content with the religious freedom they will be granted, without its public practice. It is worth noting that in the Portuguese and Spanish settlements the governors who have been bribed have allowed processions and other superstitious ceremonies to be introduced, on the pretext they were civil.

Some duties could be levied in Singor, at first modest, which could be increased when the town's population has grown sufficiently. The English did so in Madras, and it brings them 100,000 *écus* annually, with the garrison paid for.

Finally there is the concern of the [Catholic] religion. The French Missionaries will have an assured retreat there and will set up an important seminary which will have plenty to do in instructing so many different nations. From

---

[1] From Champa, the ancient Indianized kingdom engulfed by Vietnam.

there they could easily go to all the places where they have missions and learn all the languages they need.

If for good reasons which one could not foresee the site of Singor is not suitable, the King of Siam, who has guaranteed it, will be obliged to provide another, either Ligor, or Mergui, or Junk Ceylon, or even a post on the river.[1]

---

[1] That is, Bangkok on the Chao Phya. Choisy's final suggestion was the one which retained official attention. Van der Cruysse (1995) notes that the various underlinings and marginalia show this document received close ministerial scrutiny.

ABBÉ DE CHOISY

REFLECTIONS ON THE EMBASSY
TO SIAM

Extracts from the *Histoire de l'Eglise* Vol. XI (1723)
and
Mémoires pour servir à l'Histoire de Louis XIV (1727)[1]

\At the period when the King was working on expelling all
the heretics from his kingdom[2]\, a matter occurred in

[1] The title for this combination of two texts written late in Choisy's life
is ours. Choisy left, in addition to his *Journal du Voyage de Siam*
(1687), two further accounts late in his life about the Siamese
embassy. One, published the year before his death in 1724, appeared
in the eleventh and last volume of his *Histoire de l'Eglise* (1723: 207-
218). The other, written slightly earlier, appeared posthumously in
1727, in the *Mémoires pour servir à l'histoire de Louis XIV*, supposedly
printed in Utrecht but probably in Rouen. The section on Siam
appears in pp. 267-293 of the 1727 edition, and pp.142-144 and 146-
156 of the 1966 Montgrédien edition published by Mercure de
France. The passage in the *Mémoires*, which were not intended for
publication, is very similar to, but more extensive than that printed
in 1723. Here the text appearing only in the *Mémoires* is indicated by
broken brackets {...}, square brackets [...] being as usual additions by
the present editor. Sections appearing in the *Histoire de l'Eglise* but
not in the *Mémoires* passage are indicated with the backslash \...\.
However, the texts are not exactly parallel; Choisy made minor
alterations and improvements to his earlier text up to his death. The
1727 edition of the *Mémoires*, reprinted as Annex 5 to Dirk Van der
Cruysse's 1995 edition of Choisy's *Journal*, is followed here.

[2] The revocation of the Edict of Nantes, which had allowed freedom of
religious expression to Protestants, was signed on 18 October 1685,
the same day that Chaumont was addressing King Narai of Siam at
his first formal audience, seeking to persuade him to become a
Catholic.

which I shall be pardoned if I expatiate more than is customary, namely the Siamese affair. I became involved. I shall note several small details not known at all to the general public. I shall even try to repeat nothing which is in my *Journal*. I protest that I have always written the truth, but I have not always written down all that I knew. \Furthermore, I should be believed in all that I say; it is an indulgence hardly refused to contemporary authors.\ {In these Memoirs I shall hold nothing back and say everything without concealment.}

I had been staying quietly \for two months\ in the seminary of the Foreign Missions[1] when Bergeret,[2] my old friend, the principal assistant to the Secretary of State, the Marquis de Croissy,[3] came to see me, and told me in conversation that some Indian mandarins had arrived,[4] and there was talk of sending an ambassador to the King of Siam {to suggest to him that he become a Christian; he was much inclined to this, and it was an employment worthy of a clever and zealous ecclesiastic. He added that he advised me to think about this.} \It was known that this monarch, on the strength of the great reputation of our king, had sent him five or six years earlier ambassadors and magnificent presents, and that the *Soleil d'Orient*, a vessel of the [French] East Indies Company, carrying them, was shipwrecked.[5]

---

[1] The Société des Missions Etrangères de Paris was established in 1659, and soon moved to the Rue du Bac, where it remains. Choisy had withdrawn to the seminary after his illness and decision to lead a new life at the end of 1683.

[2] Jean-Louis Bergeret was a friend of Choisy; he replied to Choisy's speech on his entry into the French Academy.

[3] Charles-François Colbert, Marquis de Croissy (1626-1696), was in charge of foreign affairs from 1679.

[4] Khun Pichai Walit and Khun Pichit Maitri were sent to enquire about the fate of the missing Siamese embassy which had left Siam in December 1680; they arrived in Paris in October 1684.

[5] It probably sank off Madagascar in December 1681.

Our king, on the arrival of the mandarins, resolved to send to the king their master an ambassador to offer him his friendship and alliance, and to propose that he became a Christian. The Missionaries[1] gave out that he had much disposition to do so, that he caused churches to be built and helped the progress of [the Catholic] religion in all the neighbouring kingdoms.\ Bergeret assured me that if it depended on the Marquis de Croissy, my nomination was as good as concluded, but that because of the navy, it depended entirely on the Marquis de Seignelay.[2]

I did not need more to fire me with the apostolic ambition to go to the end of the world to convert a great kingdom. I spoke about it to Cardinal de Bouillon,[3] my friend since childhood; without losing time, he went to the Marquis de Seignelay \his friend\ to propose me. This minister told him he came too late: that the Chevalier de Chaumont, a man of quality and virtue, was named ambassador; that it had been rather difficult to find a man worthy of this mission; that the Chevalier de Nesmond[4] had been among those considered, and that two days earlier my affair would have been concluded.

The cardinal gave me this reply, but I did not lose heart; the idea of a mission was too advanced. I told him that the Chevalier de Chaumont could die during the journey, and that the embassy could fall into the hands of some sailor with little acquaintance with such matters; that [the

---

[1] It was not all the Missionaries who were guilty of such exaggeration, but one, the Missionary interpreter accompanying the Siamese envoys in 1684, Father Bénigne Vachet.

[2] Jean-Baptiste Colbert; Secretary of State for the Navy.

[3] Choisy was a playmate of Emmanuel-Théodore de la Tour d'Auvergne, Duc d'Albret (1643-1715), as he was before he became Cardinal de Bouillon at the age of 26; he was one year older than Choisy. Choisy accompanied him to the conclave in Rome in 1676.

[4] André, future Marquis de Nesmond, was a ship's captain and a Knight of Malta, who died in 1702.

Catholic] religion could suffer; that moreover the King of Siam wishing to convert, the Chevalier de Chaumont, an indifferent theologian, would give him rather superficial instruction. In short, I implored him to seek for me the coadjutancy of the Chevalier, and embassy ordinary in the case that that king undertook instruction in the Christian religion.

He spoke to the king, who agreed to my request, saying, "I have never heard before of a coadjutant ambassador, but it is justified, given the length and dangers of such a journey." {The matter being agreed, I went to Versailles to the Marquis de Seignelay to receive my instructions. I entered his antechamber at three o'clock, waited patiently until four, and began to get bored, when the Marquis de Denonville,[1] who was going as viceroy to Canada, also arrived. He had himself announced, and was told, like me, *Adesso, adesso* ["Just a moment"]. We began to talk, the one going to the East, the other to the West. Five, six and seven o'clock sounded, without our being granted an audience. M. de Seignelay was in his cabinet with Cavoye[2] and three or four other habitual companions, laughing heartily from time to time. I admired the heroic patience of the colonel of the dragoons, who perhaps was not, in truth, any more pleased than me. Finally he was called first. He stayed a quarter of an hour in the cabinet. I was called next. I do not know if an excuse was offered him for having made him wait, but I was offered not a word.}

{I left two days later against the advice of all my relatives, who put out to be greatly angered, perhaps in order not to offer me a guinea. Only the Cardinal de Bouillon gave me a thousand *écus*. Usurers provided me

1   Jacques-René de Brisay, Marquis de Denonville (1637-1710), was governor of French Canada ('New France') from 1685 to 1689.
2   Louis d'Oger, Marquis de Cavoye (1640-1716), was principal sergeant of arms in the king's household.

with the rest that I needed, and placed on my shoulders the responsibility of an enormously hazardous enterprise. They came well out of it in the end, but for me, though I came out of it alive, my financial affairs were in disorder for ten years. An ecclesiastic needs plenty of time to extract a special payment of 20,000 *livres*.[1]}

{My brother[2] reminded me of a particular horoscope which had predicted many things which happened to me, and said I would have to hunt for my fortune over the water. I did not care a fig for it and left, but I confess that, though I despise this kind of prognostication, it came back to me 4,000 leagues from here, in a storm which came very close to us in the middle of the world.}

\We left from Brest on 2 March.[3]\ Our journey began as it ended, very successfully. But we were already five months at sea, without the Chevalier de Chaumont making any overtures to me. This began to tire me. I foresaw that if this continued, I would count for nothing in Siam, when, through the partition which separated my cabin from his, I heard him pondering over his discourse [for the day of audience]. I said to him a week later (for he continued with the same song) that I had heard the most splendid things in the world. Upon that he took me into his cabin and repeated it to me; I found it faultless. From that day he began to speak to me about what had to be done in that country; I gave him my humble opinions. He is a goodly man, and truly a person of standing and quality {but he does not know geometry[4]}. I did not have much trouble in

---

1 Choisy sought funds from the Sieur de Saint-Germain, who lent him money at usurious rates; he was not free of his debts until 1695, after a long legal battle.
2 Jean-Paul de Choisy, 1632-1697, the Abbé's elder brother.
3 Actually 3 March 1685.
4 He is not learned. Choisy significantly drops his comment about Chaumont not 'knowing geometry' and later about not spitting without warning him first, from the text meant for publication.

letting him understand that, as it happened, I could be useful to him in some degree. {From that day on he did not even spit without warning me first.}

{But an interesting thought occurred to me. "If the ambassador were to die," I said, "on arrival in Siam, and I had to take over the embassy, I would have to give a discourse." No sooner said than done; I wrote the following harangue which I want to put down here to please myself. I found the original, uneven as it is, a year ago in a bundle of papers destined to be burnt. Here it is:

"GREAT KING,
The marks of esteem and friendship which Your Majesty has given the king my master, by sending him ambassadors and gifts, have touched him considerably, and though they never arrived in France, and as far as can be told suffered shipwreck, he nevertheless felt himself obliged to demonstrate his gratitude. Your Majesty doubtless knows the king my master: the European nations at your court would have given his portrait, and, though jealous of his glory, would have been forced to give justice to his merit. The whole world is filled with the echo of his name, and ambassadors from so many lands all over the globe, having sought his alliance, have returned to their own countries with their hearts and minds filled with his grandeur. It is only twenty-two years ago that he began to govern his kingdoms alone, without a [chief] minister, looking into everything himself, listening to the complaints of the dispossessed, dispensing justice to all. Each of his days has been marked by triumphs, and his soldiers have ever seen him at their head, be it in taking cities or gaining battles, they only had to follow him to be assured of victory. But after having conquered his enemies, he had to conquer himself. He stopped in the middle of his conquests, prescribing to each of the rulers in league against him what

they had to do to avoid the fury of his arms and enter into alliance with him.

It is this great monarch who sends me to the extremities of the universe to present to Your Majesty the marks of his esteem and to assure you of a constant friendship that the separation of five thousand leagues will never be capable of altering. The king my master is not limiting himself to wishing Your Majesty all happiness in this world, he further wishes you to be happy throughout all eternity. Great heroes die like other men. One needs think of this new life, the eternal life which awaits us after death, and to reach it there is but one path. One has to acknowledge, one has to love the God in heaven, the God of the Christians. Your Majesty has already received Him in your realm; you have built churches for Him; His ministers, His bishops have entered your palace. It only remains, Great King, to receive Him in your heart. He will only ask of Your Majesty facile things. He wishes that rulers be serious, just and virtuous. Has Your Majesty not already these qualities? And do you not give the example to your subjects of every virtue? It is this God which allows kings to rule with authority. It is His all-powerful arm which has sustained the king my master in his great undertakings. And when all Europe was in league to conspire in the downfall of France, this God whom we adore allowed us to win. And if our invincible monarch has laid down the law more than once to his enemies, it is by the visible protection of the God of the Christians, and we owe our victories to the piety of our king still more than to his valour.

But this great monarch does not believe his happiness complete if he cannot share it with Your Majesty. He knows Your Majesty has no need of material wealth, that your enemies fear you, that your subjects love you. He sends you, Sire, neither money nor troops, but he sends you the truth, the knowledge of the true God, the sovereign happiness in this world and the next. This is the most valuable present the king my master sends you, this is the focus of his desires. He wishes nothing more for his own glory: his victorious name throughout these years is assured of passing into ultimate posterity. It only remains to him to work at what pleases him. He likes, respects, and honours Your Majesty, and does not believe he can give Your Majesty a better indication of this than by showing you the path to heaven. This path seems to be opening to Your Majesty. For twenty years[1] you have had Missionaries and bishops capable of showing you the truth, worthy of revealing to you all the beauties of the Christian religion, a religion as old as the world, and the holiness of which makes it preferable to all others.

I hope Your Majesty will reflect on such a matter so dear to him. May it please this God, who touches all hearts which please Him, to touch that of Your Majesty, and allow you to know Him, to feel His adorable truths, so that the two greatest monarchs in the world, who are friends in spite of the seas that separate them, who, on the strength of their reputation alone, send each other ambassadors and presents, but who, it would seem, will never have the pleasure of meeting on this earth, will be able to unite in the same belief and see each other one day in heaven, in the eternal tabernacles, on those thrones of the glory which our God prepares for those who serve Him.

I have no more to wish Your Majesty. It only remains to me to present the brave Frenchmen who accompany me. They command the vessels of the king my master and make his power respected to the ends of the earth. But, as they are good subjects, they are still better Christians. They are

---

[1]   The French bishop Mgr Lambert de la Motte, Bishop of Bérythe (1624-1679), and the Missionaries established themselves in Ayutthaya in 1662.

as much heroes of the religion of Jesus Christ, ready to shed in the service of their God the same blood which they have so often given in the service of their kings. For myself, Sire, I consider I am the happiest man on earth for having completed such an important duty."}

As soon as we had arrived in Siam and I had spoken with the Bishop of Metellopolis[1] and the Abbé de Lionne,[2] I clearly recognized that things had been blown a little out of proportion, and that the King of Siam wanted to protect Christians without embracing their religion; that he did so through the policy of attracting foreigners and trade to his country, and to assure himself of some protection against the Dutch, whom all the kings in the Indies fear greatly. Mr Constance [Phaulkon], \though neither Barcalon nor prime minister but having all their functions,[3]\ confessed this \freely to me\ {in spite of himself and fell into the trap which I laid. I think I have related this fact in my *Journal*.}[4]

\We had discussions every day because, only being able to communicate in Italian or Portuguese, and the Chevalier de Chaumont understanding neither of these languages, the negotiations had to pass through me. He told me that not long before the King of Siam had been encouraged to convert to Mohammedanism by a solemn embassy from the Queen of Aceh, who rules over an important country in the island of Sumatra, and that he had given the same reply that he would undoubtedly give us.\

---

[1] Mgr Louis Laneau.

[2] Artus, Abbé de Lionne.

[3] Phaulkon, as Choisy noted in his Memorandum on Religion, refused to take the official positions, rightly fearing to create even more enemies than he already had, but placed nonentities in the posts and held all power in his hands.

[4] It was in his memorandum of on religion 1 January 1686.

\Indeed, he replied to the discourse of the Chevalier de Chaumont that he was most distressed that the King of France made such a difficult proposition which he had no knowledge of; that he craved the king's grace to consider the importance and difficulty which combine in such a delicate affair as converting from a religion that had been accepted and followed in his states for 2,229 years,[1] and that he would never forget the obligation he had to the king for all the signs he gave of his royal friendship. He redoubled his indulgence for the Christians and the Missionaries, to whom he gave complete freedom to preach the Gospels and the permission to teach the inhabitants of the country. He also added several other favours, like exempting Siamese who were Christians from [corvée] service on Sundays and holy days, and requested the ambassador to ask the king for twelve Jesuits, missionaries and mathematicians, to teach the Siamese the fine sciences of Europe, and [promised] that when they arrived in Ayutthaya and Lopburi they would find an observatory, a house, and a church.\

\After all the formal entries and all the audiences were over with the magnificence of the Indies which can scarcely be imagined (a great number of well-armed troops, 300 barges or long boats gilded to the waterline, 3,000 elephants), we began to discuss business.\ Constance suggested giving our king the town of Bangkok \which is truly the key of the kingdom\, on condition troops, engineers and money were sent. The Chevalier de Chaumont and I did not think such a thing feasible, and we told him {frankly} that the king would not wish to pledge himself on his word to the extent of spending four or five million which would perhaps be lost.

---

[1] Buddhism was that ancient, but had certainly not been the religion of Siam for that long, and indeed Siam proper only emerged in the thirteenth century.

Things would have stayed there {and I think he would not have thought more of it without my taking a retreat at the seminary in Siam to prepare myself for receiving holy orders.[1] Some matters arose which Mr Constance wished to discuss with the Chevalier de Chaumont. An interpreter was needed. He used Father Tachard,[2] and found in him a gentle, supple, compliant and yet bold if not to say reckless character. He spoke to him of the idea he had, the idea which we had treated as a chimera.} \The Jesuit\ Father Tachard undertook to bring about a successful conclusion to the proposal. He told Mr Constance that we had no credit at court, in which he was not far wrong, and if he wished to write to Father de La Chaize[3] about it, His Reverence would bring it to fruition. \Enough is known about this affair to know that it did not succeed.\

{Whilst these things were being negotiated, Mr Paumard,[4] a Missionary, who was always at Mr Constance's house, got wind of this and came to warn me. But I did not wish to abandon my retreat and let Father Tachard get on with it, who, in doing so, pinched a fine golden crucifix which the King of Siam was going to give me at the farewell audience, and to which the good Father was treated in justice since the Chevalier de Chaumont and I were only actors on stage after that, and he was the real ambassador charged with secret negotiations. I was not fully aware of all this until after my return to France. But when I was back once more in my own good country, I was so pleased that I felt no rancour towards anyone.}

[1]   Choisy was consecrated priest in Lopburi by the Bishop of Metello-polis on 10 December 1685.

[2]   Guy Tachard, (1651 or 1648-1712), entered the Order of Jesuits when young and taught mathematics. He was to play an equivocal role in this and the subsequent French embassy of 1687.

[3]   Father de La Chaize, sometimes de la Chaise, 1624-1709, was Louis XIV's powerful Jesuit confessor.

[4]   Etienne Paumard was a confidant of Phaulkon practising medicine.

\It is true,\ I have \often\ said good things about Mr Constance in my *Journal*, and nothing which was not true; he was one of the people with the greatest wit, liberality, magnificence, and intrepidity in the world, full of great concepts, but perhaps he only wished to have French troops to declare himself king on the death of his master which he foresaw as coming very soon. He was proud, cruel, pitiless, and with outrageous ambition. He supported the Christian religion because it could support him, but I would never have trusted him in matters in which his own betterment was not involved.

\We brought back on our return three ambassadors of the King of Siam, and magnificent presents of gold and silver vases, porcelain, and japanned work. The second ambassador had been in China, and the king his master had selected him to compare the two countries.\

{On arriving at Brest[1] I learnt two very different pieces of news. One was that Mr Boucherat[2] was chancellor; I was very pleased. The other was that the Cardinal de Bouillon was exiled; I was much put out. The Chevalier de Chaumont and I left at once and travelled together the first day. He was forever looking at the ladies of Brittany and confessed, with all his devotion, that he found them as beautiful as the Princess of Conti.[3] We had come from seeing Siamese ladies. He arrived first at Court, as he should; I arrived three days later. We were lionized.}

{The king asked me many questions. He asked one in particular which was much talked about. He asked me how one said 'eat' in Siamese; I told him *kin*. A quarter of an hour later, he asked me how one said 'drink'; I told him

---

[1]   The embassy returned to Brest on 18 June 1686.
[2]   Louis Boucherat (1616-1699) was named Chancellor of France on 1 November 1685, succeeding Michel Le Tellier who had just died.
[3]   Martie-Anne de Bourbon, Princess of Conti (1666-1739), daughter of Louis XIV and Louise de La Vallière, was a court beauty.

kin.[1] "That's got you," he said. "You told me just now that *kin* meant 'eat'." "That's true, Sire," I replied without hesitation, but in Siamese *kin* means 'to swallow'; and to say 'eat' one says *kin kaou*, 'swallow rice', and *kin nam* 'swallow water'." "At least," said the king, laughing, "he gets out of it wittily." I told the truth, and wit had nothing to do with it on this occasion.}

{The following day, while walking in the gallery, I heard Cavoye, Livry[2] and other courtiers saying that the King of Siam had sent presents to the Cardinal de Bouillon. That caused me a lot of chagrin. I had intended to suppress them, thinking the occasion unfavourable. I was afraid the king would learn about this from others rather than me. I ran to the Marquis de Seignelay; he was at Sceaux.[3] I went to seek the counsel of the chancellor, who advised me to go and tell the king without losing a moment. I went to find the Count of Auvergne[4] who advised the same.}

{I returned to the gallery, and as the king was going to hear mass, I came close to the royal ear and said, "Sire, I beseech Your Majesty to grant me a moment's audience in your cabinet." He replied, "Is it urgent?" I replied, "Yes, Sire." "Very well," he said, with his sun-like look, "come after my lunch." I did not fail to, and took up post in the antechamber when he passed by. He tapped my arm lightly and said, "Follow me." I entered his cabinet, where he was alone, and said to him, "Sire, I believe I am obliged to inform Your Majesty that the King of Siam has written to the Cardinal de Bouillon and sent him some presents."

---

[1] Choisy might better have said *derm*.

[2] Louis Sanguin, Marquis de Livry (1646-1723), was principal maître d'hôtel of Louis XIV.

[3] The château de Sceaux was the stately mansion belonging to Seignelay.

[4] Frédéric-Maurice de La Tour d'Auvergne was a brother of the disgraced Cardinal and Duke de Bouillon.

"How so?" he interrupted me. "And who advised him to do so?" "Sire," I replied, "I did. I thought I did well to have a great monarch honour the first almoner of Your Majesty and the leading divine in France." He turned round rather quickly and said, with a look enough to send me a hundred feet beneath the earth, "You did that on your own initiative!" "Sire," I replied, "I spoke about it to the Chevalier de Chaumont and he approved my action, not being able to guess that the Cardinal de Bouillon would be sufficiently unfortunate to displease you. Your Majesty had just granted him the Abbey of Cluny.[1]" "That's enough!" he said, turning his back to me; I left his cabinet.}

{The courtiers wanted to compliment me on my audience, but I pretended modesty and moved on quickly. I went to lock myself in a small room in a teahouse where, without reproaches, I thanked God for humiliating me. I had been too proud, I thought I had pulled off a master-stroke during my journey by pleasing both the Jesuits and the Missionaires. The king's recent look soon stopped my cackle. I thought, though, that my innocence could put me at ease.}

{At seven in the evening I left my lair and returned to the palace to see if M. de Seignelay had not returned. I found on arrival twenty people who told me the king had sent for me everywhere to speak to me. I went to M. de Seignelay's rooms; he was ready to eat me. "Really, sir," he said, "the king is in a terrible temper. Why did you not come to see me first?" I told him I had gone in search of him, and not finding him, the Count of Auvergne advised me to go straight to the king. He asked for the letter the King of Siam had written for the Cardinal de Bouillon and the list of the presents; I put everything in his hands.}

---

[1] The Abbey of Cluny was one of the richest in the patronage of the monarch.

{I went in the evening to the king's supper as usual, but he said nothing to me: no more questions. My friends warned me that the king seemed much angered with me on retiring for having interfered where I had no business to, and even with the poor cardinal whom he accused of having sent me to Siam in order to acquire some presents for himself, he who had not the least thought of this. I thought it best to let the storm blow over, and I went to Paris to lock myself up in my seminary where an hour of prayer in front of the holy sacrament allowed me to forget everything which had happened to me.}

{Six months later I presented the king with *The Life of David* and the *Psalms*[1] which he received very graciously. I was obliged to Father de La Chaize who had spoken to him in my favour and who arranged an audience in his cabinet. His Majesty had realized that I was not greatly to blame, so much so that he gave me leave the following year to go and visit the cardinal who was at Tarascon and very sick, and said he was very pleased that certain people went to see him in that condition. Alas, the good monarch had perhaps a good opinion of me, and he had reason to have such at that period. I was still fresh from my oriental mission where I had not failed to absorb some of the [Missionary] fervour just in seeing it in action, though paying relatively little attention to it.}

{A month after my arrival in Paris, the ambassadors of the King of Siam arrived.[2] The king paid all their expenses and} gave them audience[3] in the great gallery at Versailles. {A magnificent throne was installed there. They delivered a very fine discourse which the Missionary Abbé de Lionne

---

[1] *Interprétation des Psaumes avec la Vie de David* was published by Choisy in 1687 and dedicated to Louis XIV.
[2] The solemn entry into Paris took place on 12 August 1686.
[3] The audience was held on 1 September 1686.

translated into French. They showed the king marks of respect which almost approached adoration, and when all was over did not wish to turn their backs towards him but left retreating backwards.}

{The presents which they had brought were lined up in the room at the end of the gallery. M. de Louvois,[1] who did not think much of things in which he had no part, was extremely disdainful of them. "My dear Abbé," he said in passing, "all that you have brought, is it really worth fifteen hundred *pistoles*?" "I have no idea, sir," I replied very loudly, so everyone would hear me, "but I know for a fact that there is more than twenty thousand *écus* of solid gold there, not counting the workmanship. And that is leaving out the japanned cabinets, the screens, and the porcelain." He gave me a disdainful smile, and someone passed who apparently gave an account of this fine conversation to the king, for that very evening Mr Bontemps[2] asked me, on behalf of the king, if what I had told M. de Louvois was true. I gave him the proof by presenting him with a precise memorandum of the weight of each gold vase, which I had drawn up in Siam before leaving. I am sure that this was subsequently checked.}

{This trifling incident did not lessen M. de Louvois' irritation with me. Already he did not like me because I counted among the friends of his adversary the Cardinal de Bouillon. Four days later, he recounted in front of everyone at table at Meudon a story about me which was false from beginning to end, in which the archbishop of Paris[3] also

---

[1] François Michel Le Tellier, Marquis de Louvois (1639-1691), was son of Chancellor Michel Le Tellier, and Minister of War.

[2] Alexandre Bontemps (1626-1701) was the principal valet de chambre to Louis XIV.

[3] François de Harlay-Champvallon (1625-1695) was archbishop of Paris from 1671 and a friend of Choisy.

figured large. The archbishop learnt about this, sent for me, told me everything and said: "My poor Abbé, let us not call attention to calumny; that is the way to kill it."}

{I shall say nothing more of the Siamese ambassadors. Books have been printed about their witty remarks,[1] and in truth the first ambassador[2] had much intelligence. He looked after us in Siam; he occupied the functions of gentleman in ordinary, more or less. I told Mr Constance that this person seemed to me capable of being a success in France. He told me he had not a sufficiently high rank to be charged with such a fine embassy, and that, moreover, he was very annoyed with the court, because on the death of his brother the Barcalon[3] two million had been taken from him. I replied that one could give him higher title, and the benefits would cause the hurts to be forgotten. He thought about it, spoke about it to the King of Siam, made him Ok-phra and ambassador. One must however admit that Mr Constance was right. This good ambassador on his return entered the Petracha camp,[4] and through his advice contributed a lot to make him king, and cut poor Mr Constance in two.[5] He is at present Barcalon, that is to say prime minister.}

The discourse which he gave before the king at his farewell audience was admired. {I was given the honour of being suspected of having had a hand in it. The king sent for me to ask for it; he wanted to show it to Mme de

---

[1]   Donneau de Vizé in the *Mercure Galant* published four special volumes devoted to the activities and dicta of the ambassadors.

[2]   The chief ambassador, Ok-phra Wisut Sunthorn, more commonly known as Kosa Pan.

[3]   The *Phra Klang* Kosathibodi.

[4]   Petracha, foster-brother of King Narai, led a coup against him in May 1688, and after Narai's death in July declared himself king.

[5]   Phaulkon was arrested on 18 May 1688, tortured for two weeks, and cut into pieces on 5 June at Thale Chupson near Lopburi.

Maintenon.[1] I brought him a draft which happened to be in my pocket. He ordered me to bring him a well-penned copy on his return from the hunt, which I did. The truth is that the ambassadors had put in their tongue a part of the thoughts it contained.} The Abbé de Lionne had translated this into French, {Mr Tiberge[2] gave it that simple, natural, and noble turn of phrase which he knows how to give everything he touches, and I put in a few full stops and commas.} You may be pleased to see it again here:

"GREAT KING

We come here to seek Your Majesty's permission for us to return to the king our master. The impatience with which we know he is consumed to learn of the success of our embassy, the marvels which we have to relate to him, the precious tokens which we will bear him of the singular esteem that Your Majesty has for him, and, above all, the assurance that we are able to give of the royal friendship which has been eternally sealed with him; all this, still more so than the winds and the seasons, invite us to depart, while the good reception which we have received here on all sides on the orders of Your Majesty would be capable of making us forget our country, and we might dare say the very orders of our monarch.

But, on the point of distancing ourselves from your royal person, we have no words left which are capable of

---

[1] Françoise d'Aubigné, Marquise de Maintenon (1635-1719). She married the poet and novelist Scarron but was widowed in 1660 and put in charge of the education of the offspring of Louis XIV and Mme de Montespan. After the death of his queen, Maria-Theresa of Austria, in 1683, Mme de Maintenon became Louis XIV's secret wife and exercised much influence over him, particularly in religious matters.

[2] Abbé Louis Tiberge was one of the superiors in the seminary of the Foreign Missions.

expressing the feelings of respect, admiration, and gratitude with which we are imbued. We were well prepared to find in Your Majesty greatness and extraordinary qualities: the reality has fully justified this and indeed far surpassed our expectations. But we are obliged to confess to you that we did not expect to find the accessibility, the gentleness and affability which we have met. We did not consider either that qualities which appear so contradictory could appear in the same person, and that one could bring together so much majesty and so much kindness. We are no longer surprised that your people, too happy to live under your empire, demonstrate everywhere the love and tenderness they have for your royal person.

For us, Great King, overwhelmed by your blessings, charmed by your virtues, touched to the bottom of the heart by your goodness, astonished at the sight of your profound wisdom and of all the miracles of your reign, our life seems too short, and the whole world too small, to publish what we think. Our memory will be taxed to retain so many things; that is why we have avidly gathered in faithful registers all that we could observe[1] and we shall finish them with the sincere protestation that though we have noted much, still much has escaped us. These memoirs will be preserved for posterity and placed in safety among the most rare and most precious stately objects. The king our master will send them as presents to the princes his allies, and in that way the East will soon know, and all the centuries will come to learn, of the incomparable virtues of Louis the Great. We shall finally carry away the happy news of the perfect health of Your Majesty, of the care that

---

[1]   The ambassadors' secretaries wrote down every detail of things seen, even counting the trees in the parks visited. Only one fragment survives.

Heaven has taken to continue the course of a life which should never end."

{This discourse, which was greatly applauded, was followed by sixteen others which the ambassadors gave the same day to the princes and princesses of the royal household. There were full of good sense and wit.} I shall add that which they gave to the Duke of Burgundy:[1]

"GREAT PRINCE

who will ever be the ornament of the whole universe, we are going to prepare in the Orient the paths of fame by which will be carried in a few years the account of your victories and your great actions. If we are still alive then the testimony which we shall give to what we discovered in you will cause to be believed all that, in your exploits, appears unbelievable. 'We have seen', we shall say, 'this prince when still a child; and even then his entire character could be seen on his forehead and in his eyes, we judged him capable of doing one day what he is today doing.' What will overwhelm the king our master with joy will be the assurance that we shall give him that the Kingdom of Siam will find in you a solid support for the friendship which we have come to contract with France."

{I also found among my papers the neat compliment that they paid to the Duke of Berry:[2]

"GREAT PRINCE

To whom Heaven reserves victories and conquests; we shall have the advantage to carry to the king our master the

---

[1]   The eldest son of the Dauphin, then aged four; he died in 1712, and it was his son who succeeded Louis XIV in 1715.

[2]   He was born the day before the solemn audience of 1 September 1686; he was just four and a half months old when this speech was addressed to him. He died in 1714, one year before his grandfather, Louis XIV.

first news he will ever have had of you; and we shall fill him with joy in telling him of the happiness we had to know you from birth and the happy augury which was derived from the embassy for your future grandeur. We hope that your reputation will follow us swiftly, and soon pass over the waters after us, to spread happiness in a court and in a kingdom where you will always receive all due honours."}

{Madame the Dauphiness gave birth to the Duke of Berry shortly after the arrival of the Siamese ambassadors. A *Te Deum* was sung in Notre Dame. The chancellor and the bishops complained that the life guards were not under arms in their presence, but Sainctot[1], the master of ceremonies, told them that the life guards were only dancing attendance on the chancellor, and that for the gentlemen clergy they only bore arms when they went as a body to the kings's audience. There was that evening a great ball at the Town Hall, which the Siamese ambassadors did not wish to attend, saying that they had not yet paid all their visits to the royal house, and that their duty had to take precedence before their pleasures.}

\After the return of the Chevalier de Chaumont, the Jesuit Father Tachard presented the propositions that Constance, prime minister of the King of Siam, had made to us and which we had rejected: to send to Siam ships, troops, officers, and armaments, and he would deliver the town of Bangkok to them.\

\Father de La Chaize, thinking these propositions advantageous to [the Catholic] religion, passed them on to the king, who accepted them, and the following year he sent La Loubère, a gentleman of intelligence and merit, as envoy extraordinary, and Desfarges, the king's lieutenant

---

[1]   Nicolas Sainctot (1623-1713) was master of ceremonies and later the person who introduced ambassadors.

from the Brissac[1] regiment, to command the troops. They arrived without mishap and entered Bangkok. But soon jealousy took hold of the Siamese, and the king fell sick, Petracha, the general commanding the elephants, revolted, seized the king's person and left him to die tranquilly, had Constance cut down in the middle of his person, and beseiged, or rather blocked Bangkok, which the French only left when provisions ran out. An honourable capitulation was arranged and vessels were provided to return to France. This enterprise cost our king more than four million. \

\Petracha, now King of Siam, imprisoned Constance's wife; she was Japanese and very beautiful[2]. The eldest son of the king[3] fell in love with her, but could not deflect her faith or her virtue. She was freed after four years[4], and given the superintendancy of the confectionary, an important post in a country where such products are greatly appreciated. \

---

[1]   General Desfarges was the King's lieutenent at Brisach, now Breisach am Rhein in Germany.

[2]   Maria Guyomar de Pinha had a part-Bengali part-Japanese father and a Japanese mother, Ursula Yamada, with some Portuguese admixture. She was imprisoned by Petracha after the coup of 18 May 1688, escaped, and sought refuge in the French fort in Bangkok, but was ignominiously handed back to the Siamese by Desfarges. She remained in prison until the death of Petracha in 1703.

[3]   Sorasak, who was notoriously cruel. He acceeded to the throne accredited with the name Sua (Tiger) on the death of his father and died in 1709.

[4]   She was not freed until Petracha died.

INDEX
of persons, places, and *ships*

More *Treasures from the Past*

TREASURES FROM THE PAST

A PILGRIMAGE TO
ANGKOR
PIERRE LOTI
TRANSLATED BY
W. P. BAINES · MICHAEL SMITHIES

A Pilgrimage to Angkor
Pierre Loti
Translated by W. P. Baines and Michael Smithies
ISBN 974-7100-26-6

1996. 107 pp, 145x210 mm, 22 color plates. Baht 295, US$ 9.95

This travel writer and exotic novelist was both a member of the French Academy and a career naval officer who as a child had wanted to visit Angkor. He was finally able to realize his dream in 1901 during a short leave. He writes with a vivid pen recalling the jungle ruins and a reception given for him in the palace in Phnom Penh. This fascinating short work of Loti's maturity, out of print in English for more than sixty years, is again available, now in a revised translation.

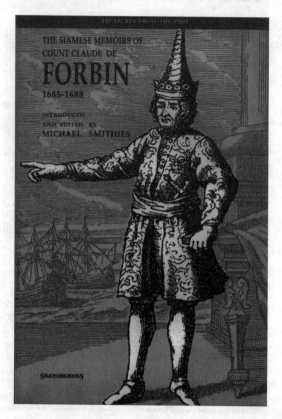

The Siamese Memoirs of Count Claude de Forbin, 1685-1688

Introduced and edited by Michael Smithies

ISBN 974-7100-30-4

1996. 190 pp, 145x210 mm, 25 b/w illus. Baht 325, US$ 10.50

Chevalier Forbin (later a count) came to Siam at the age of 29 as an aide-de-camp in the French embassy of 1685. He pleased King Narai, who made him general of the king's armies and governor of Bangkok, but he had to contend with the jealousy of the powerful Levantine minister Phaulkon. In these memoirs written at the end of his long life, he looks back on his time in Siam, tells of his experiences at the courts of Narai and Louis XIV, and describes how the French adventure in Siam ended.

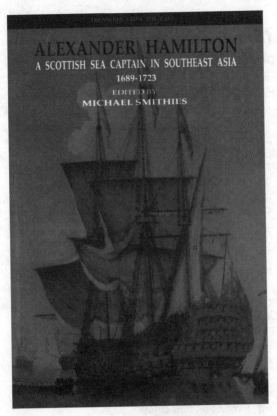

Alexander Hamilton:
A Scottish Sea Captain in Southeast Asia 1689-1723
Edited by Michael Smithies

ISBN 974-7100-45-2

1997. 206 pp, 145x210 mm, 22 b/w illus. Baht 325, US$ 10.50

Alexander Hamilton's classic text, *A New Account of the East Indies*, has only been published three times since it first appeared in Edinburgh in 1727. Its length and breadth (it covers everywhere from the Red Sea to Japan) have precluded more editions, and the most recent, the Argonaut Press limited 1930 edition, is unobtainable. Hamilton was one of the very few persons to come to Siam in the eighteenth century and leave an account of his stay. Editor Michael Smithies has taken the fourteen chapters covering Southeast Asia in Hamilton's account and provided an introduction and explanatory footnotes to the selection, with modernized spelling. This new edition of a frequently cited but rarely seen text comes with contemporary illustrations.

More from Silkworm
Titles on Southeast Asian History

SOUTHEAST ASIA

Southeast Asia: An Introductory History
Seventh Edition
Milton Osborne
ISBN 974-7100-47-9
1997. 263 pp, 140x215 mm, index. Baht 520, US$ 16.75

Southeast Asia: Past and Present
Revised Fourth Edition
D. R. SarDesai
ISBN 974-7100-39-8
1997. 422 pp, 153x233 mm, index. Baht 750, US$ 19.95

Southeast Asia in the Age of Commerce 1450-1680
Volume One: The Lands below the Wind
Anthony Reid
ISBN 974-7047-57-8
1994. 274 pp, 155x235 mm, 61 b/w illus. Baht 475,   US$ 15.50

Southeast Asia in the Age of Commerce 1450-1680
Volume Two: Expansion and Crisis
Anthony Reid
ISBN 974-7047-58-6
1994. 405 pp, 155x235 mm, 64 b/w illus., index. Baht 575,   US$ 18.50

The Comfort Women
George Hicks
ISBN 974-7047-40-3
1995. 265 pp, 140x215 mm, 21 b/w photos, index. Baht 495,   US$ 14.95

THAILAND

Burma-Thailand Railway
Edited by Gavan McCormack & Hank Nelson
ISBN 974-7047-21-1
1993. 175 pp, 145x205 mm, 11 b/w photos, index. Baht 225.00,   US$ 6.95

Forest Recollections: Wandering Monks in Twentieth-Century Thailand
Kamala Tiyavanich
ISBN 974-7100-40-1
1997. 384 pp, 152 x 230 mm, index. Baht 750, US$ 24.00

Siam Mapped: A History of the Geo-Body of a Nation
Thongchai Winichakul
ISBN 974-7047-46-2
1994. 272 pp, 155x235 mm, 32 color plates, 5 b/w illus., index. Baht 495, US$ 15.95

Studies in Thai History
David K.Wyatt
ISBN 974-7047-44-6
1994. 306 pp, 145x215 mm, index. Baht 450, US$ 14.50

Thailand: A Short History
David K.Wyatt
ISBN 974-7047-44-6
1994, 351 pp, 145x205 mm, 13 maps, index. Baht 375, US$ 12.25

CAMBODIA

Facing the Cambodian Past, Selected Essays 1971-1994
David Chandler
ISBN 974-7047-74-8
1996. 331 pp, 145x210 mm, index. Baht 450, US$ 14.50

A History of Cambodia
Second Edition
David P. Chandler
ISBN 974-7047-09-8
1993, 287 pp, 150x230 mm, 3 maps, index. Baht 420, US$ 14.00

The Khmers
Ian Mabbett and David Chandler
ISBN 974-7100-27-4
1995. 289 pp, 150x225 mm, 47 b/w photos, 8 maps, index. Baht 450, US$ 14.50

The Tragedy of Cambodian History:
Politics, War, and Revolution since 1945
David P. Chandler

ISBN 974-7047-07-1
1994. 396 pp, 160x240 mm, 3 maps, index. Baht 550, US$ 17.75

NORTHERN THAILAND

A Brief History of Lan Na, Civilizations of North Thailand
Hans Penth
ISBN 974-7047-29-2
1994. 74 pp, 145x215 mm, 31 b/w photos, 1 map. Baht 125, US$ 4.00

Chiang Mai Chronicle
D.K. Wyatt & Aroonrat Wichienkeeo
ISBN 974-7047-67-5
1995. 264 pp, 175x245 mm, 13 maps, index. Baht 595, US$ 19.50

*Jinakalamali Index: An Annotated Index to the Thailand Part of
Rattanapañña's Chronicle Jinakalamali*
Hans Penth
ISBN 974-7047-32-2
1994. 358 pp. 135x215 mm, 2 maps. Baht 550, US$ 18.00

Ordering Information

Prices are subject to change without notice. All orders must be accompanied by check, money order, or credit card information.

Postage and handling costs are free of charge for delivery within Thailand. For overseas orders, the cost is US$ 7.00 for the first book and US$ 2.50 for each additional copy for surface mail only. Please allow 8-12 weeks for delivery of overseas orders.

For foreign orders, please use the US dollar price.

Method of payment

We accept payment by international bank draft, VISA, and MasterCard. For credit cards, please include card number, expiry date, and cardholder name and address. For international bank drafts, please add US$ 12.00 or £ 8.00 for clearing fee.

Mail, fax, or e-mail your order to:

Silkworm Books
P. O. Box 76, Chiang Mai 50000, Thailand.
Fax +66 (53) 27-1902
E-mail: silkworm@pobox.com